Friends and Family:

More Critters to Color

By Robin Joy Andreae

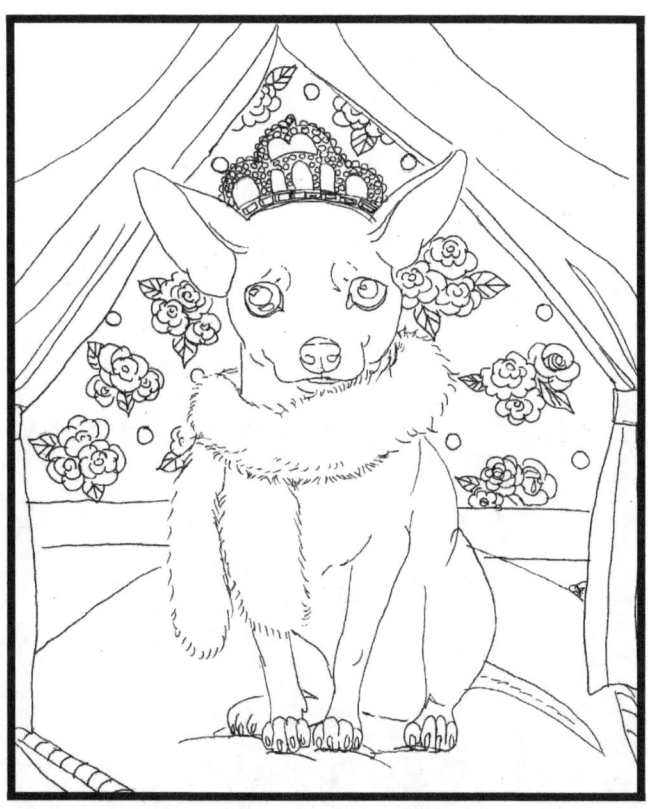

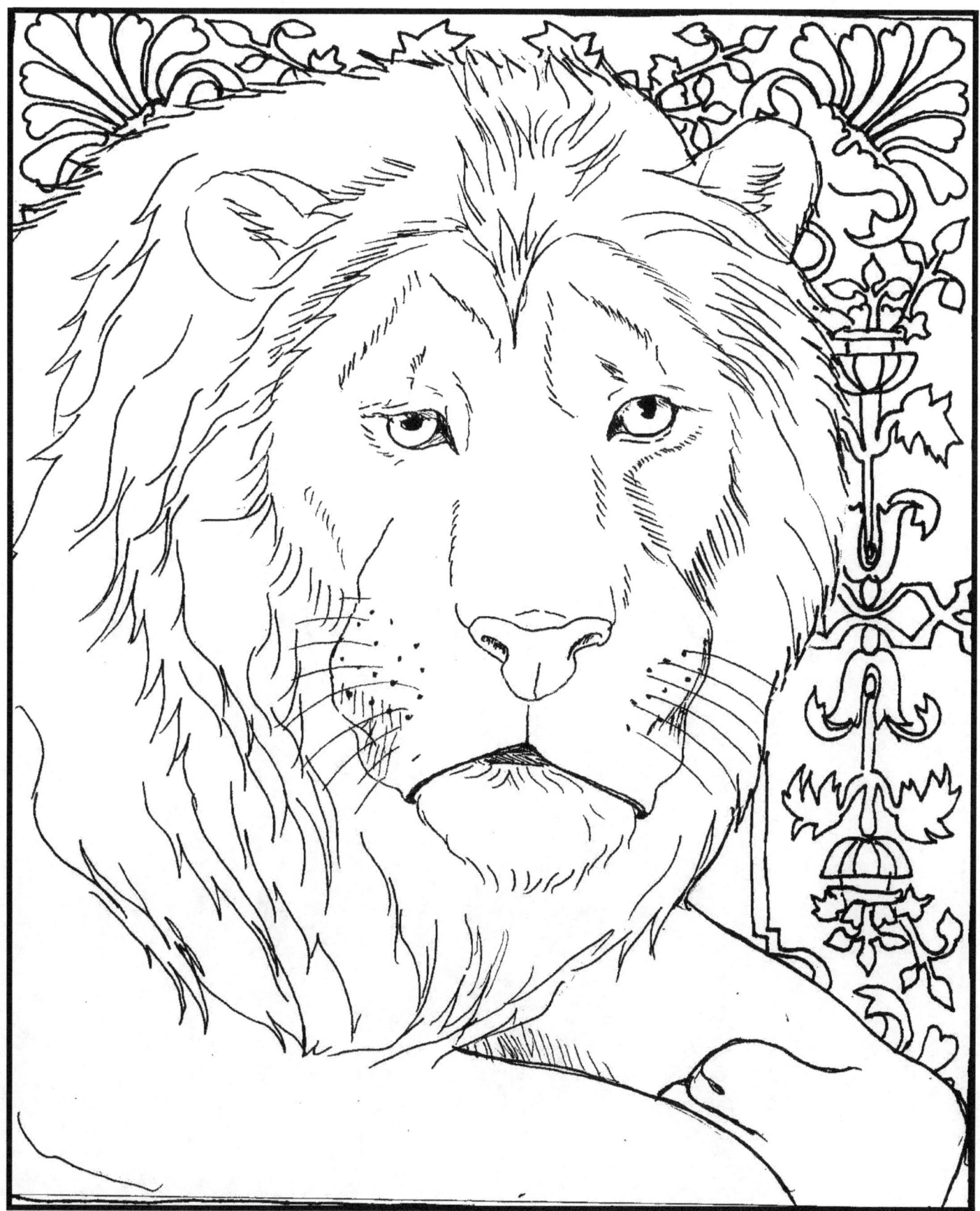

Figure 1 African Lion

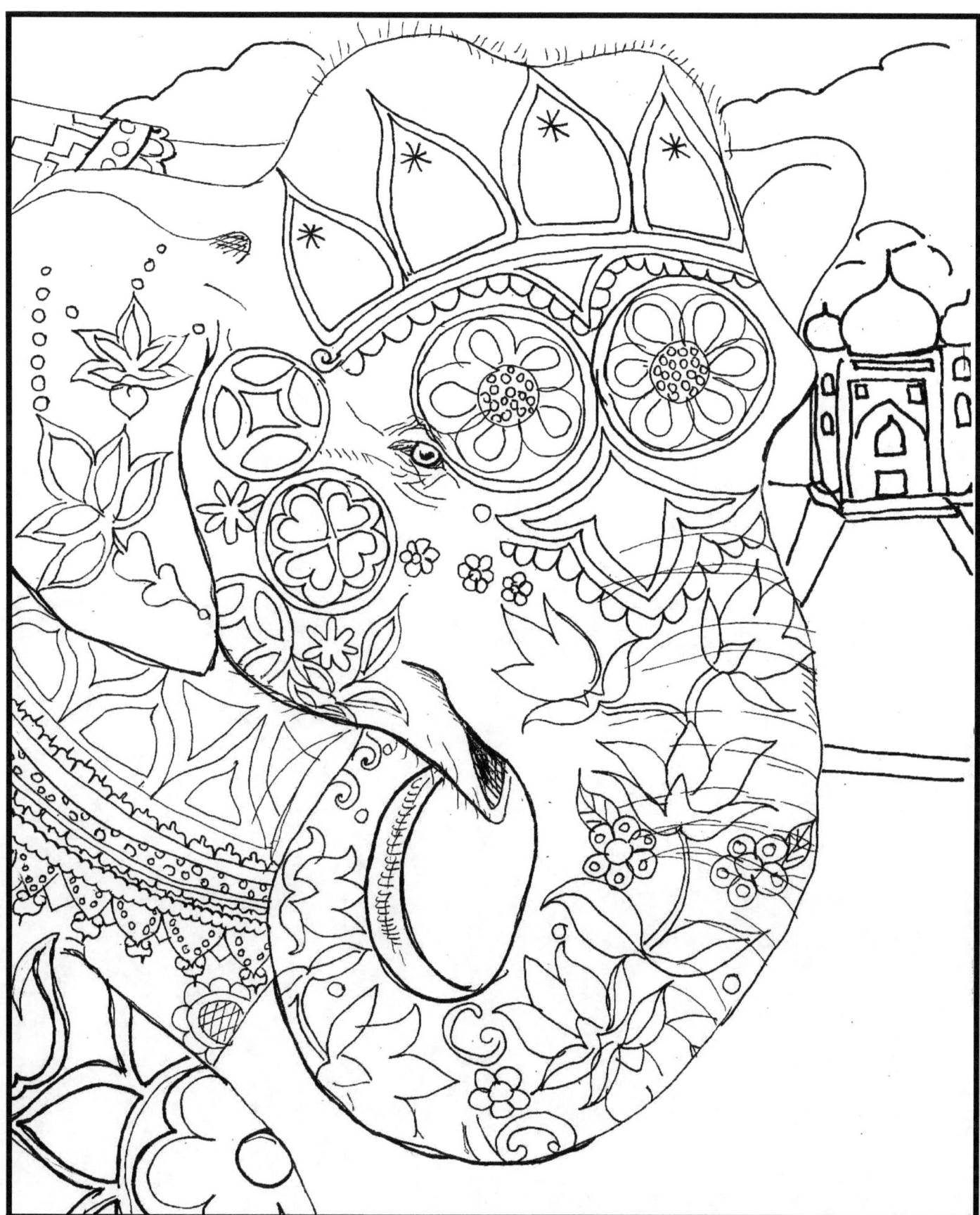

Figure 2 Asian Elephant

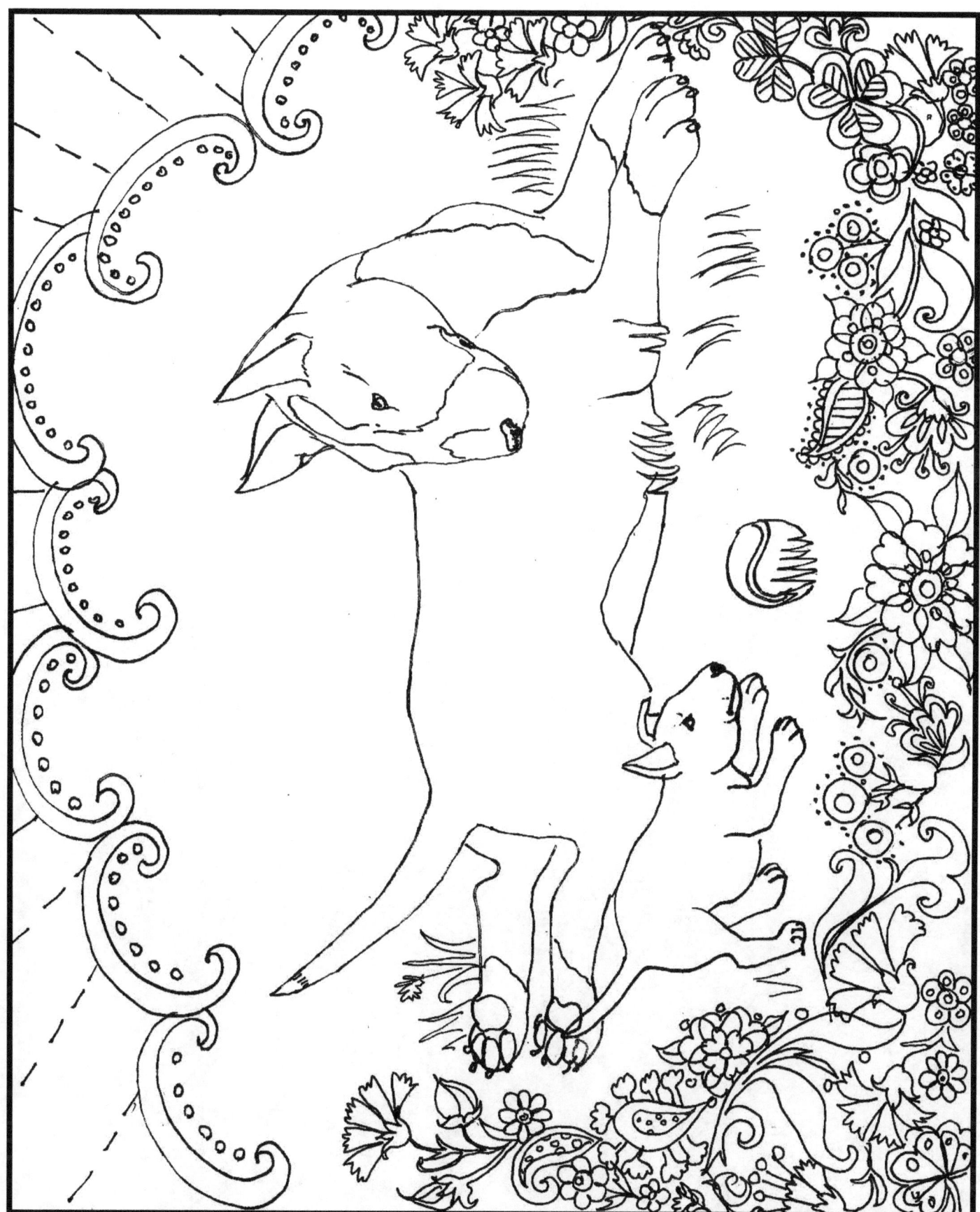

Figure 3 Bull Terrier

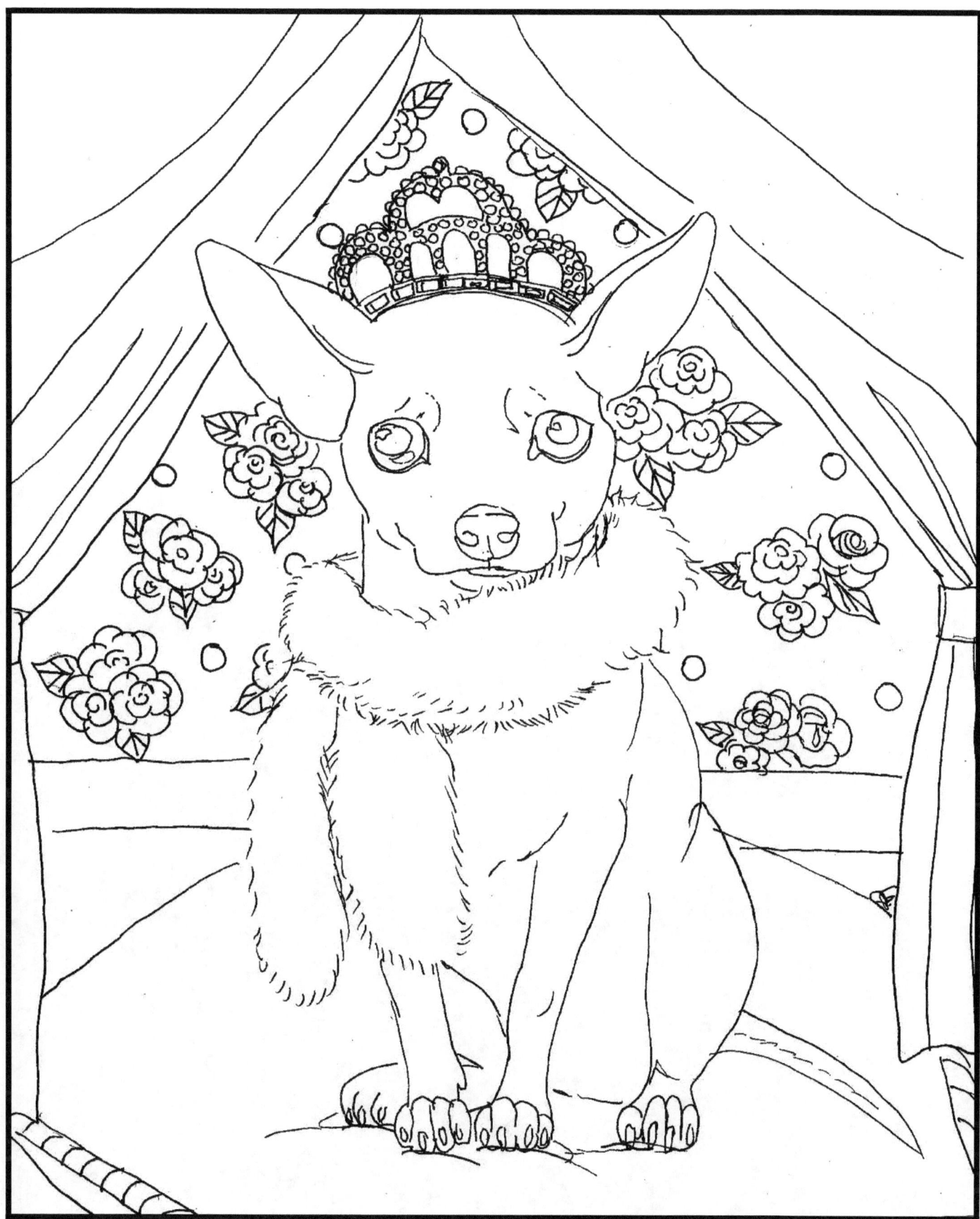

Figure 4 Princess

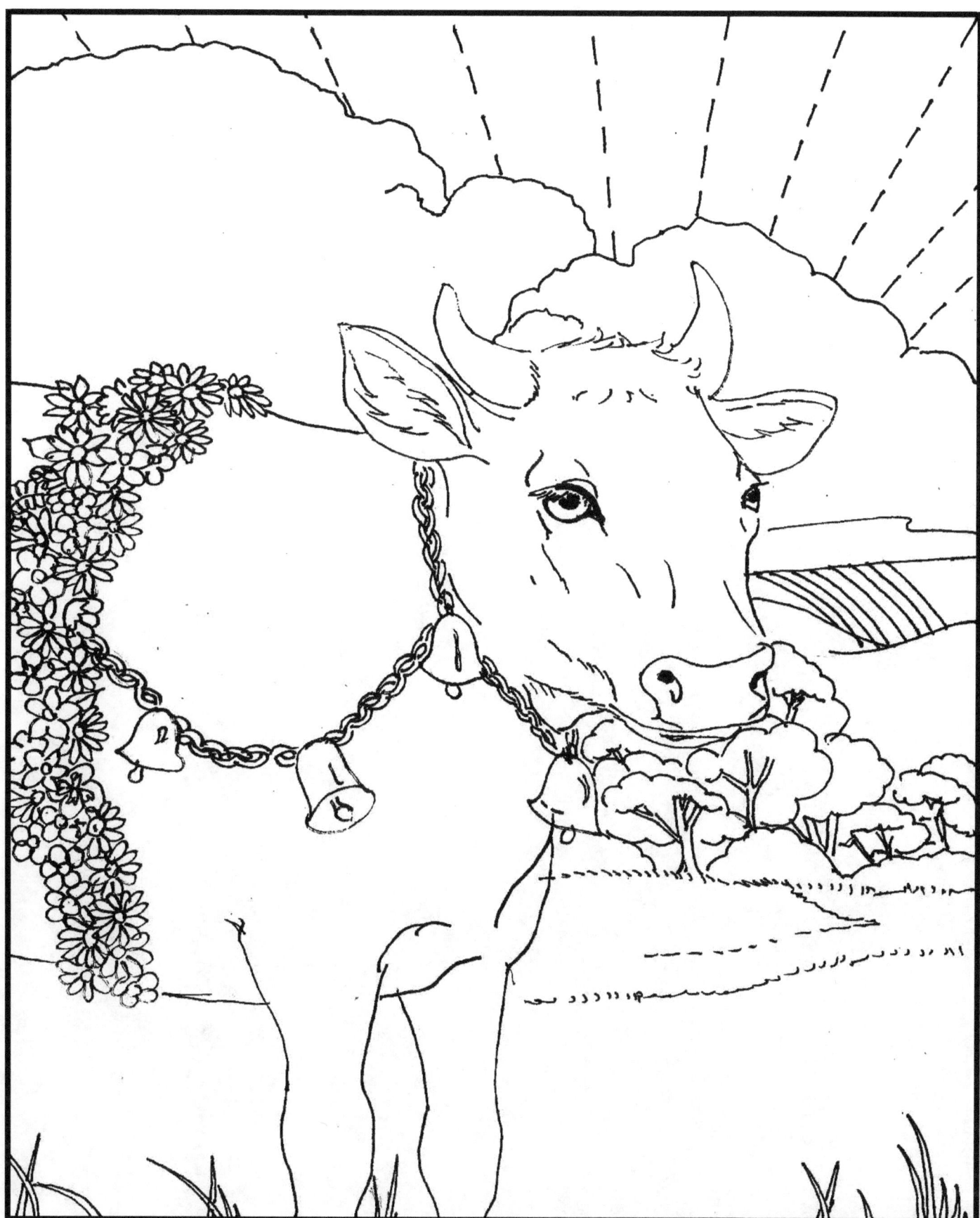

Figure 5 Sunshine

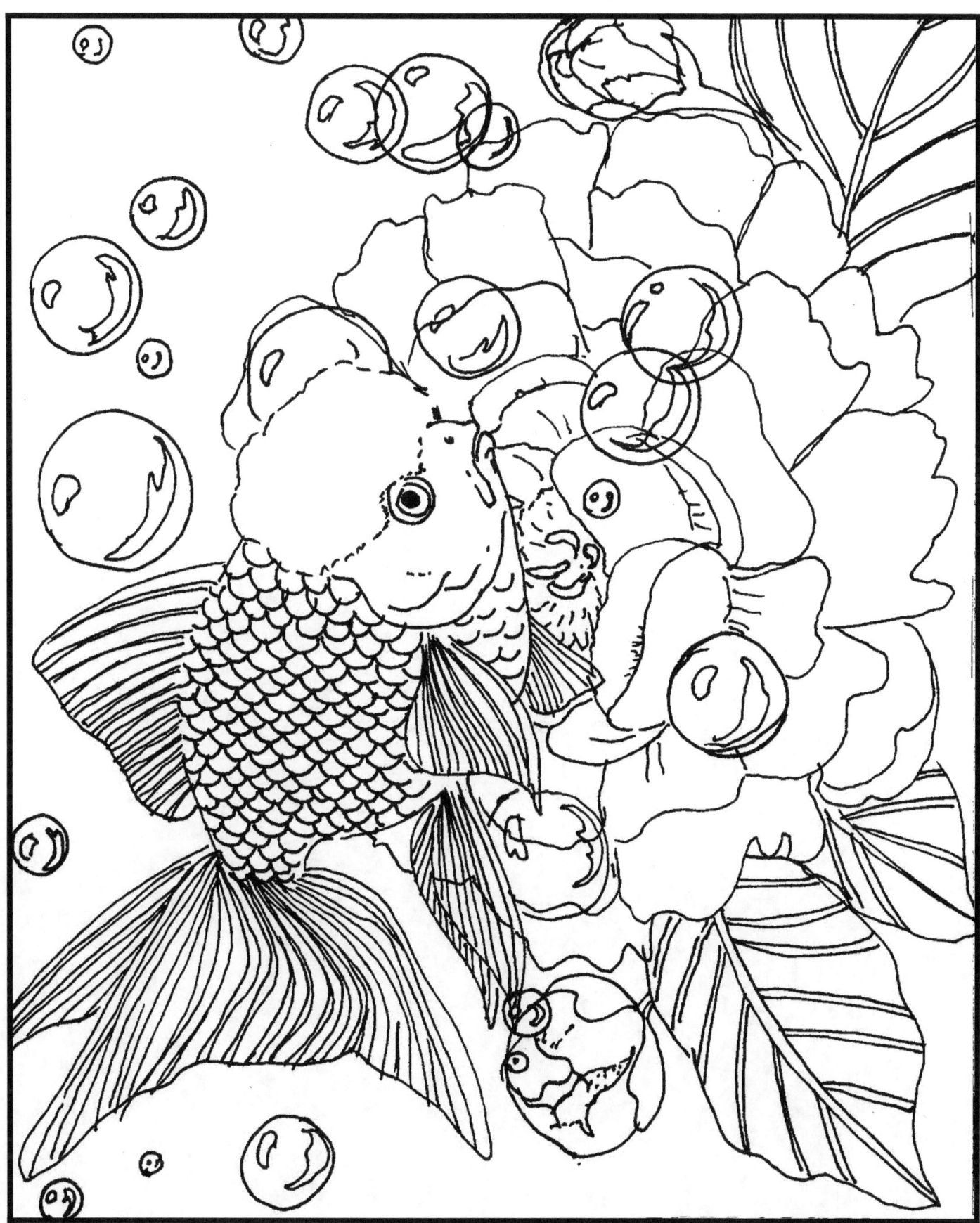

Figure 6 Oranda Goldfish

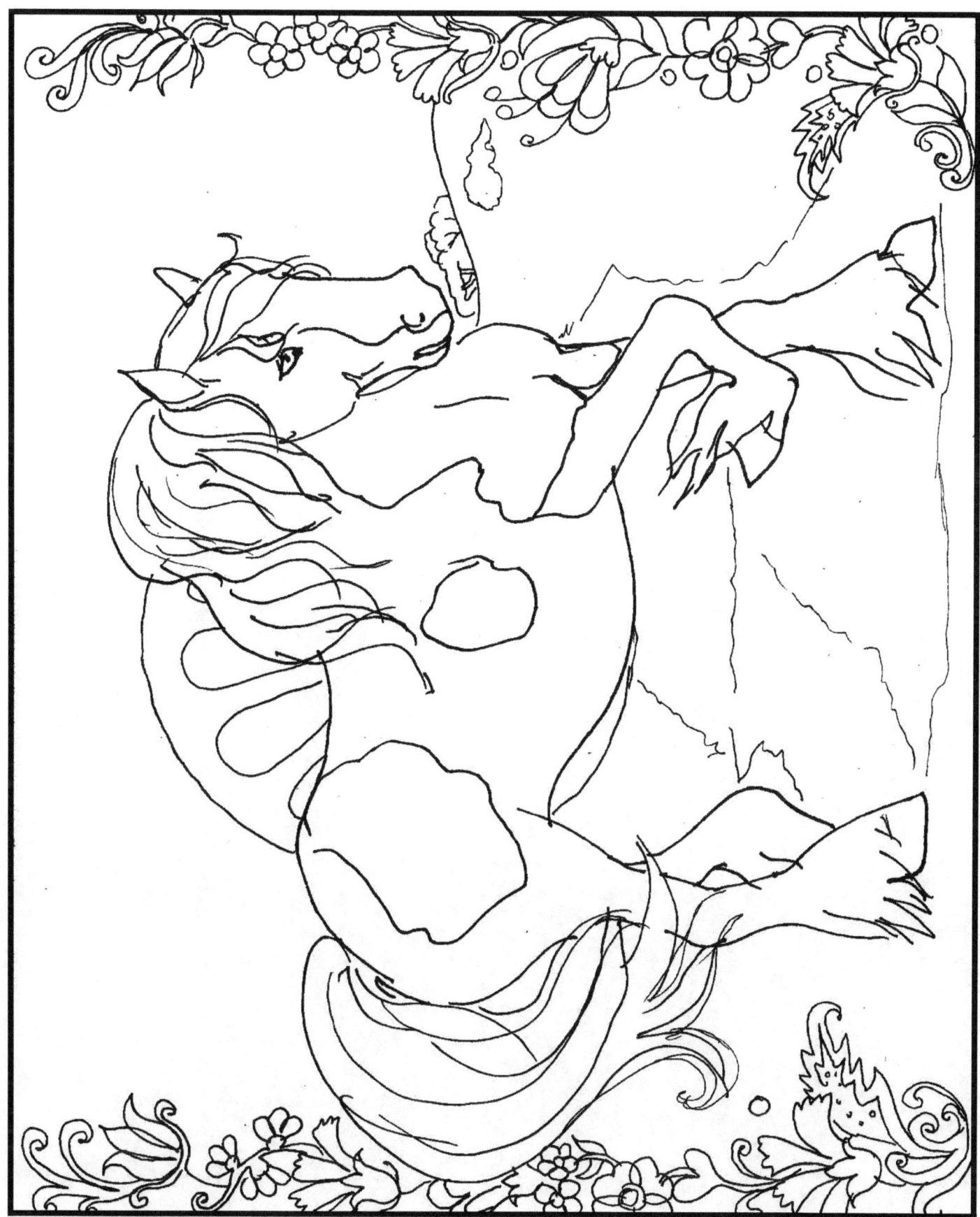

Figure 7 Gypsy Vanner, Roma Beauty

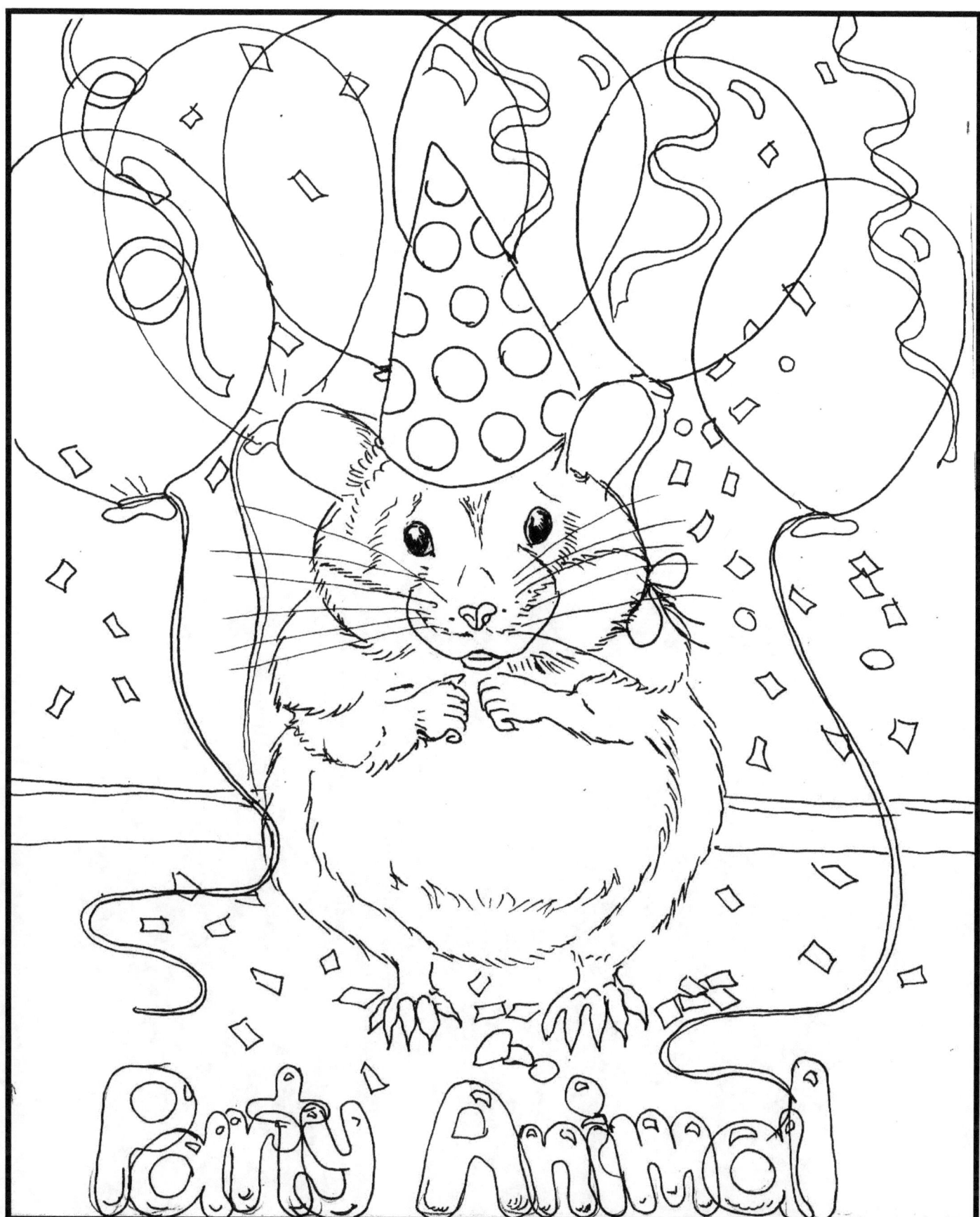

Figure 8 Party Animal

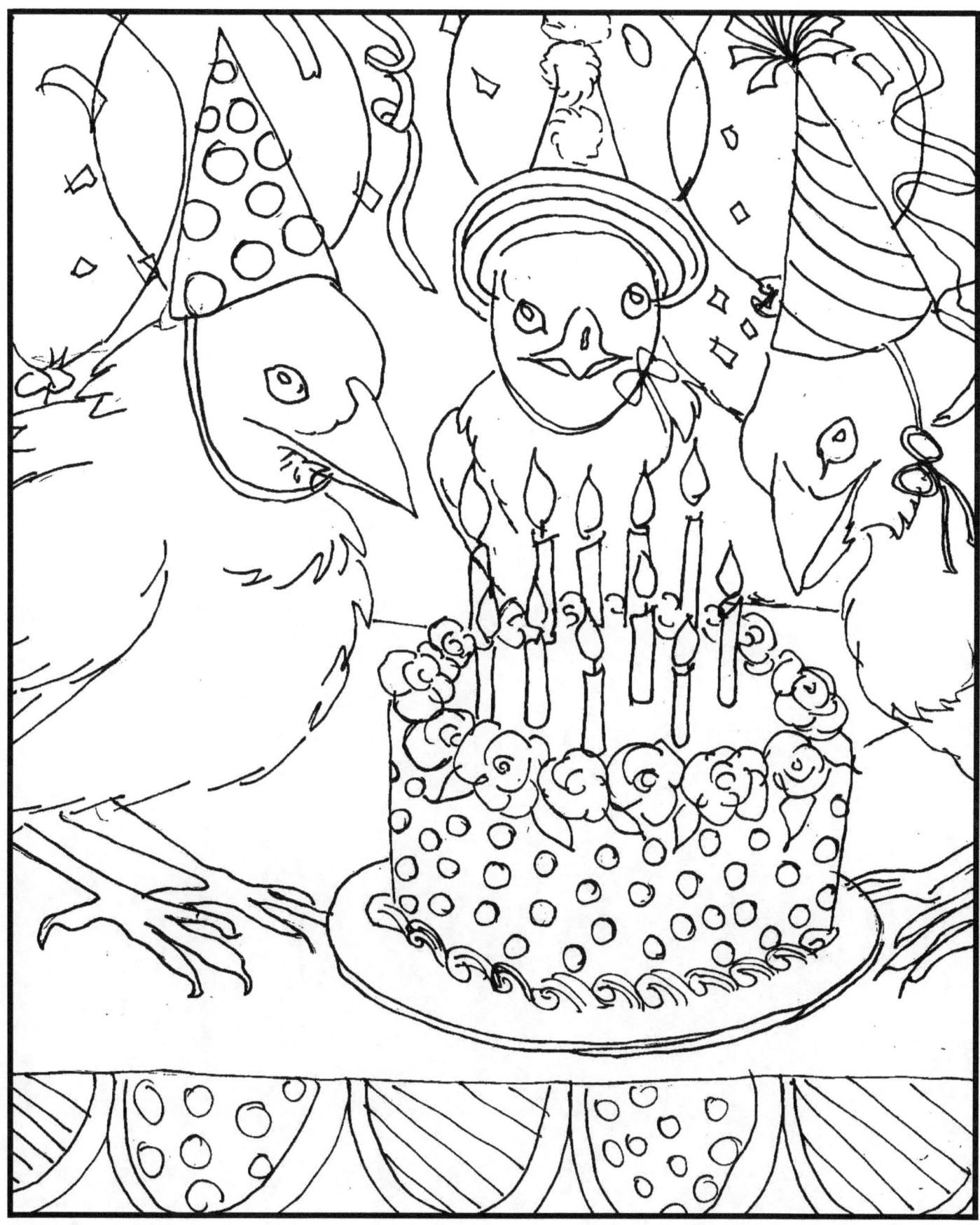

Figure 9 Bird Day Party

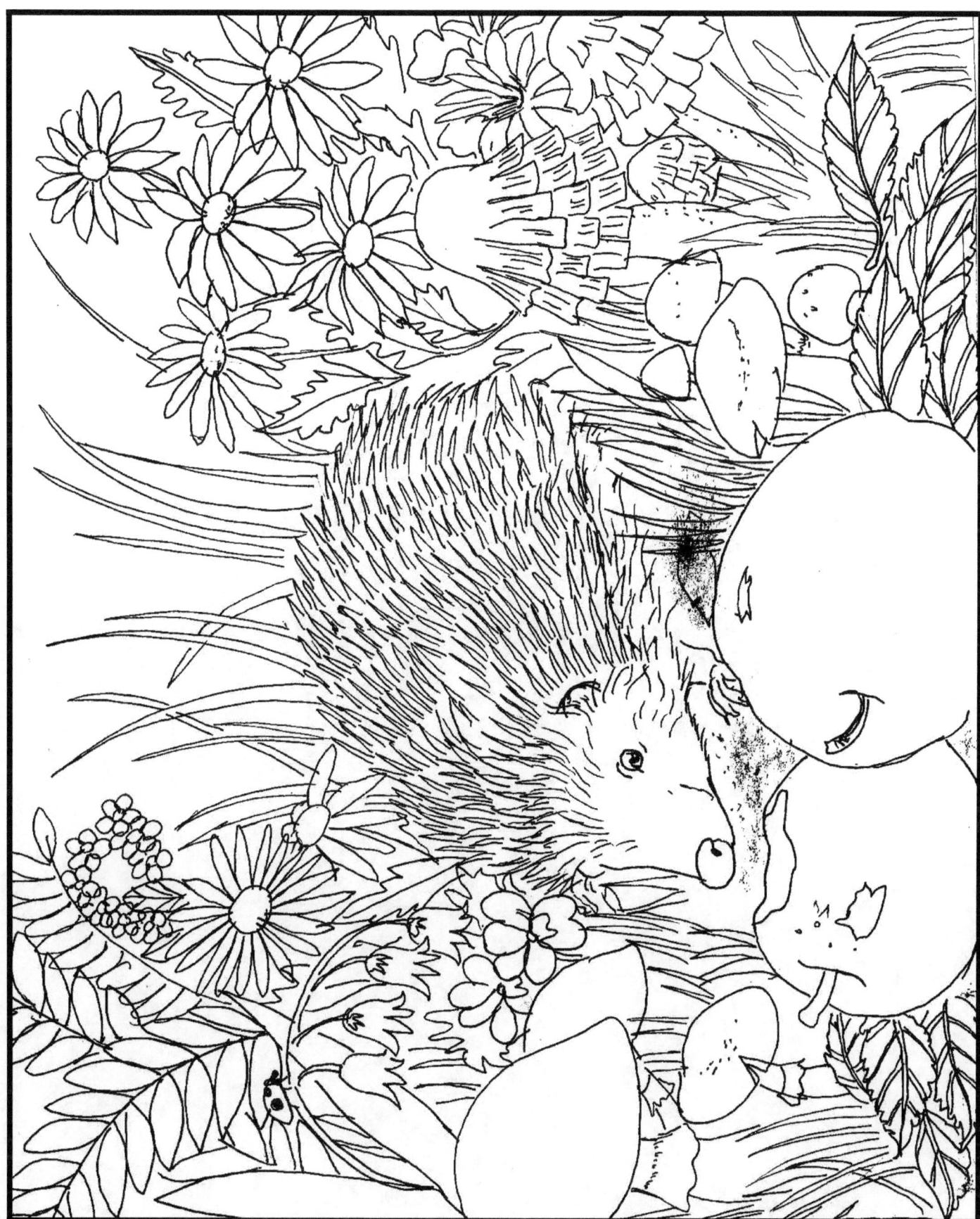

Figure 10 Hedgehog's Treasure

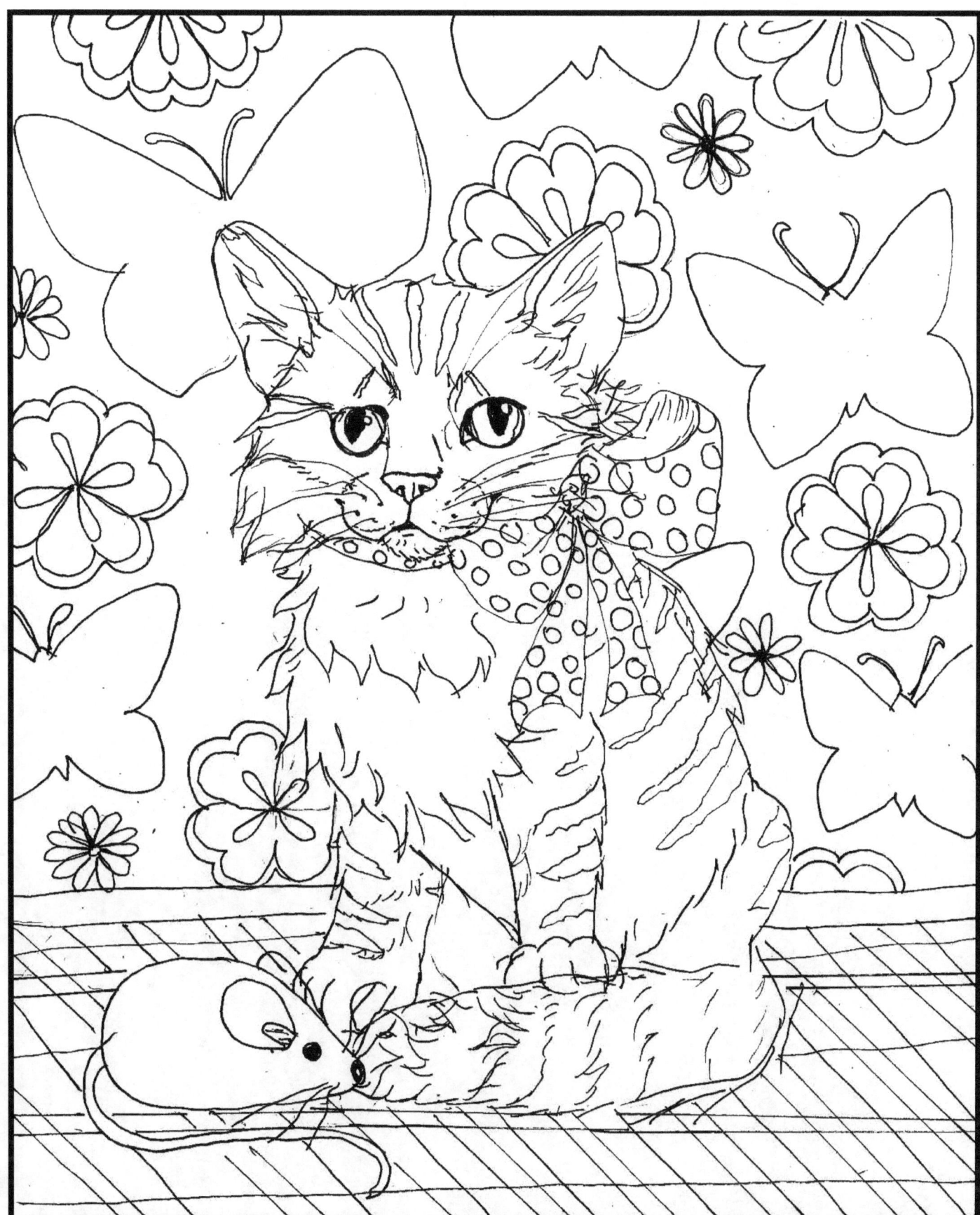

Figure 11 Kitten

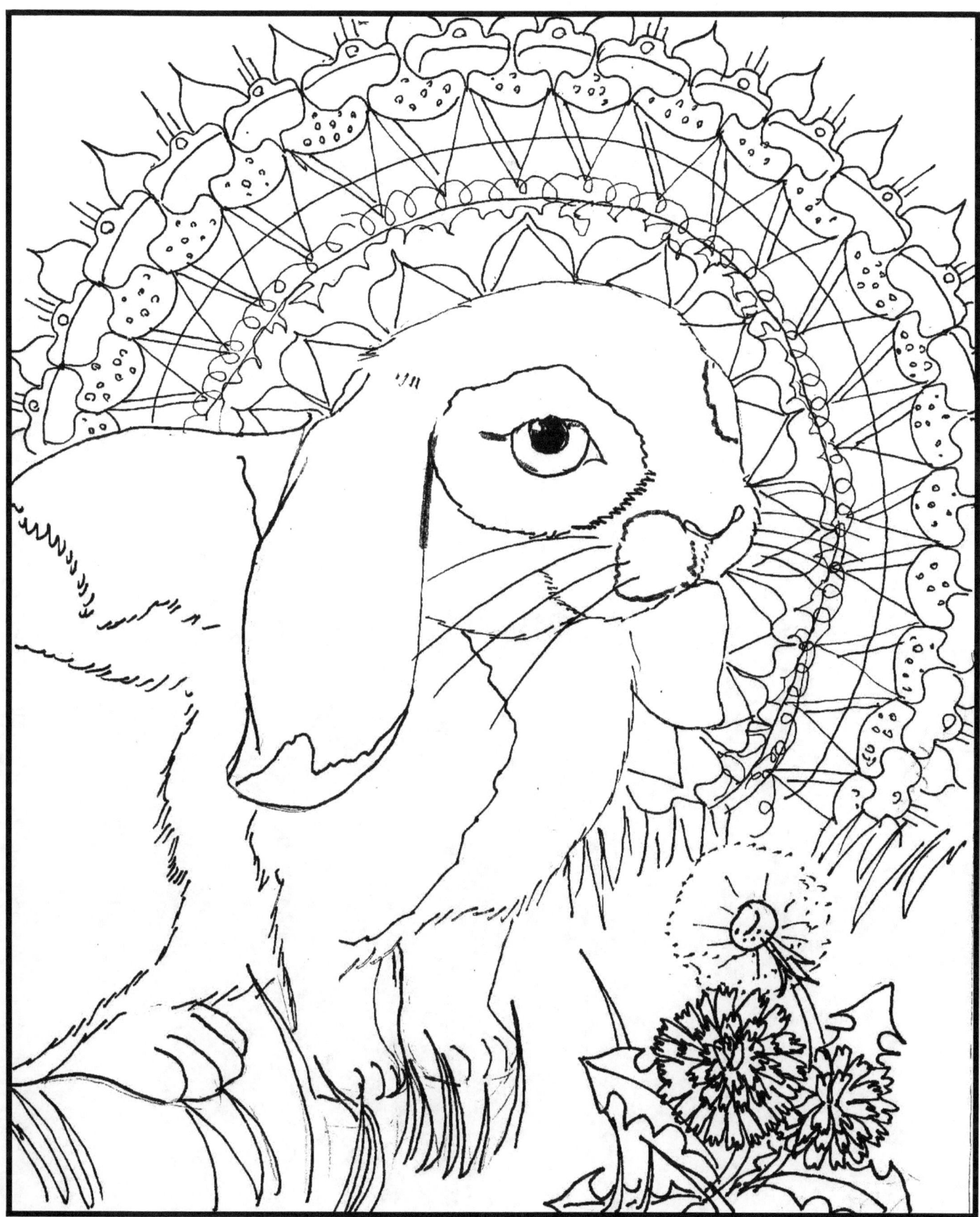

Figure 12 Lop Eared Bunny

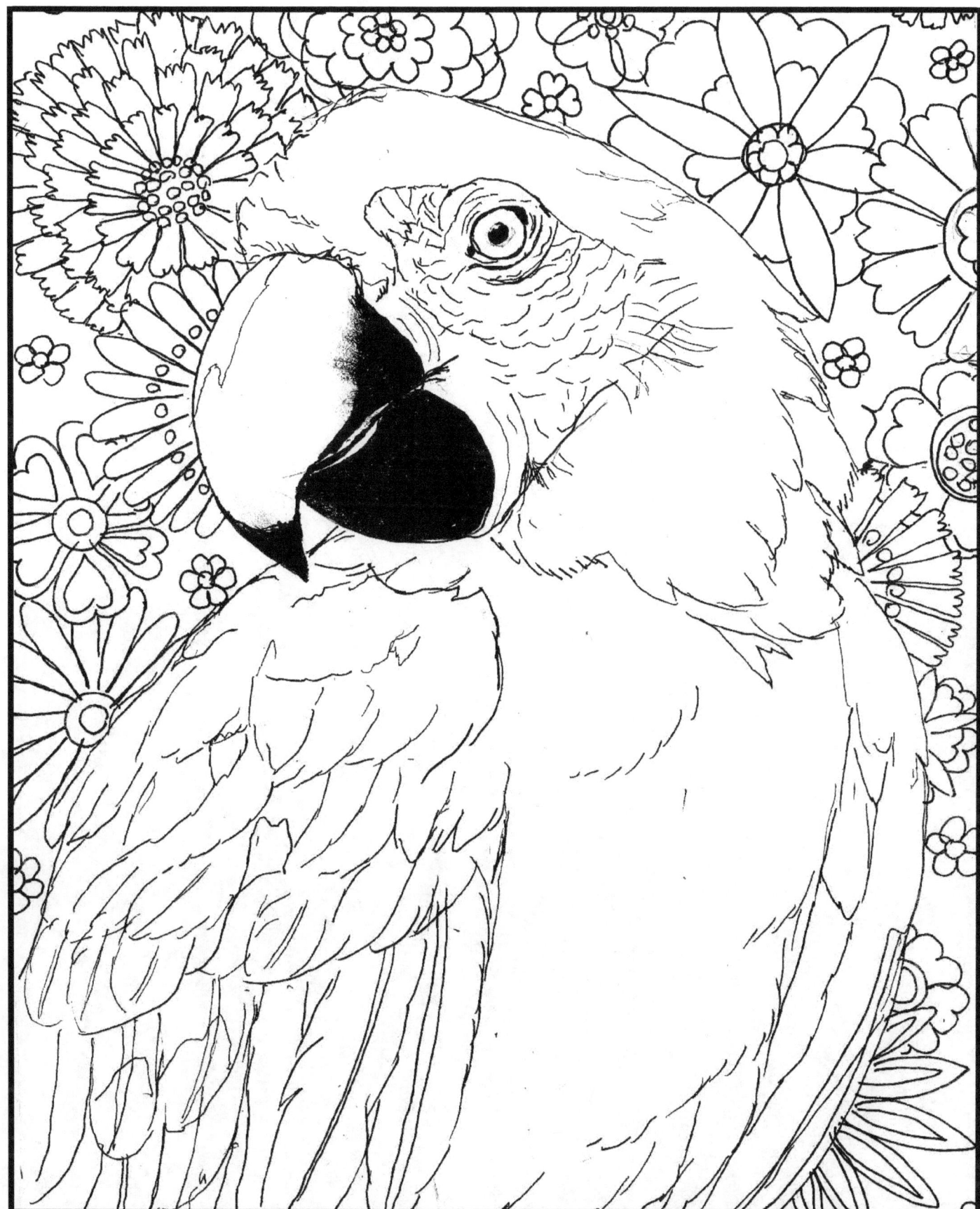

Figure 13 Macaw

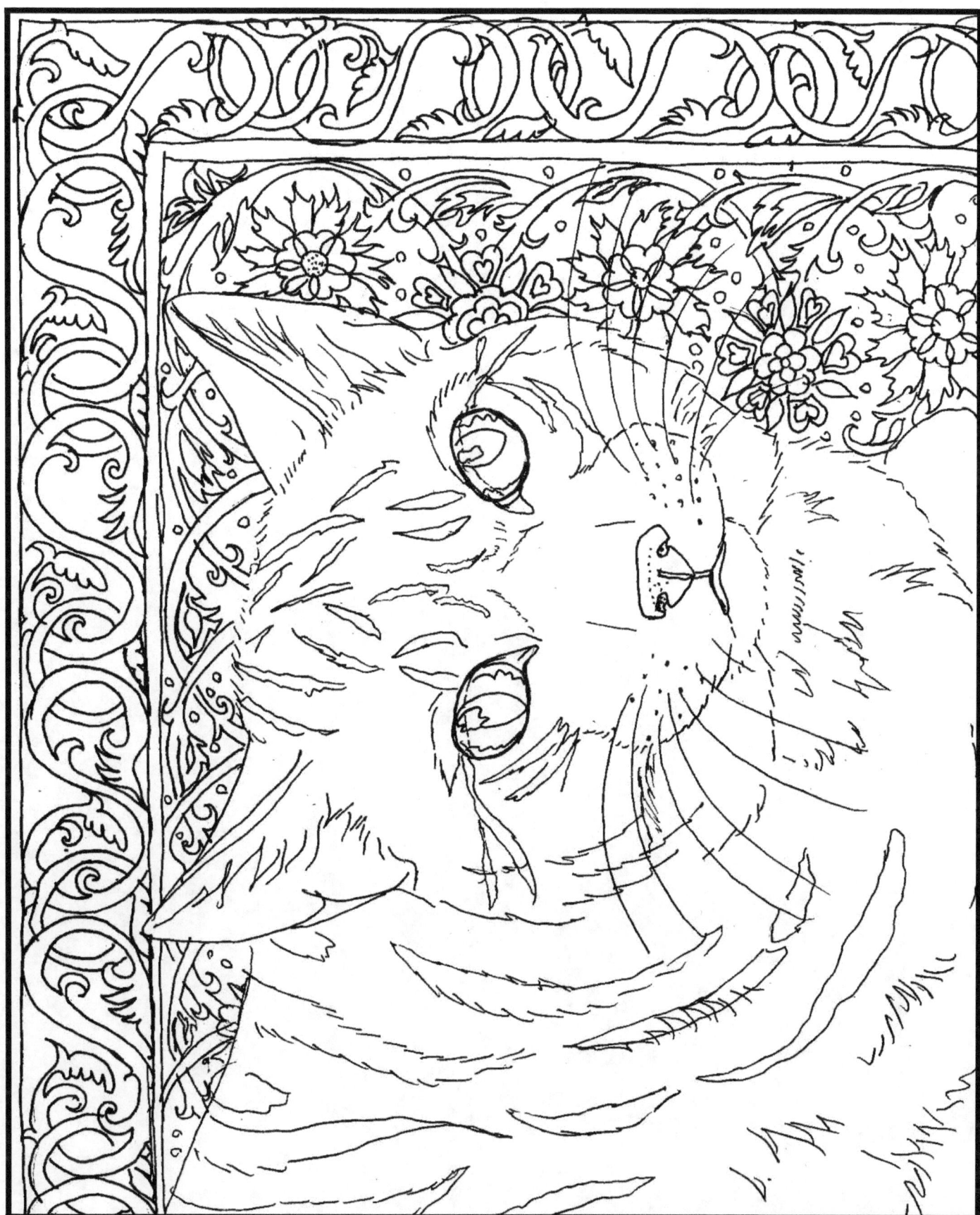

Figure 14 Tabby Cat

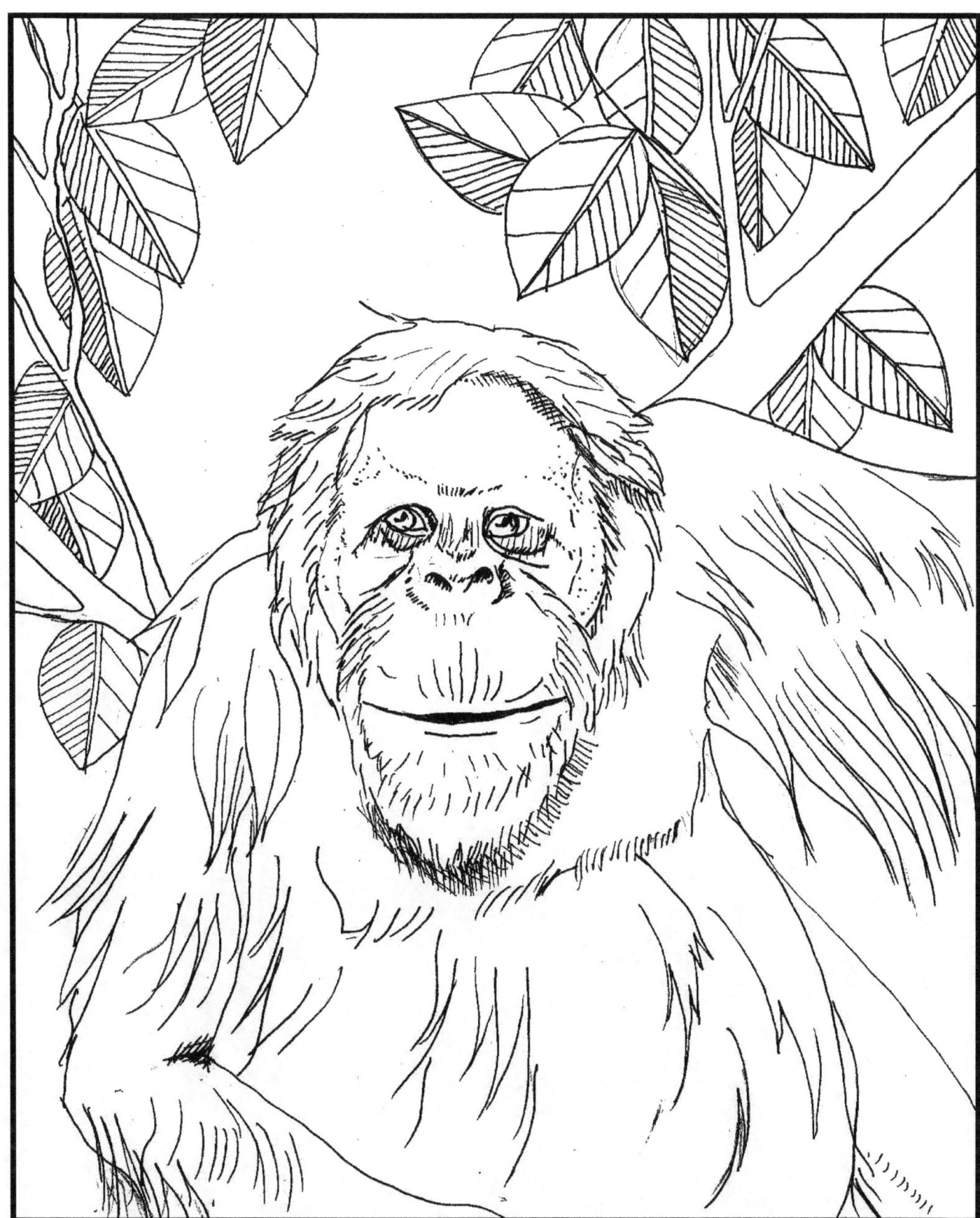

Figure 15 Orangutan

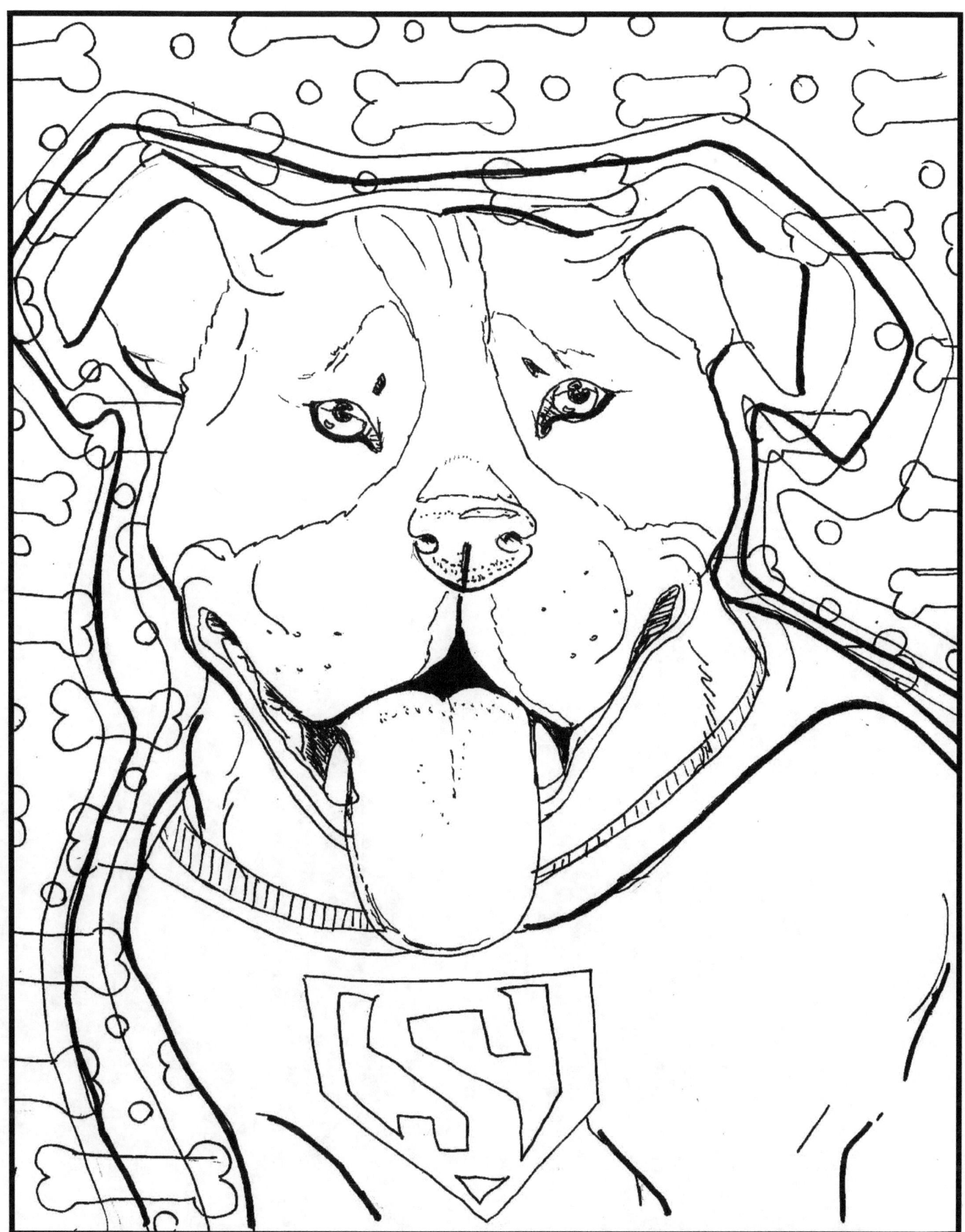

Figure 16 Super Dog

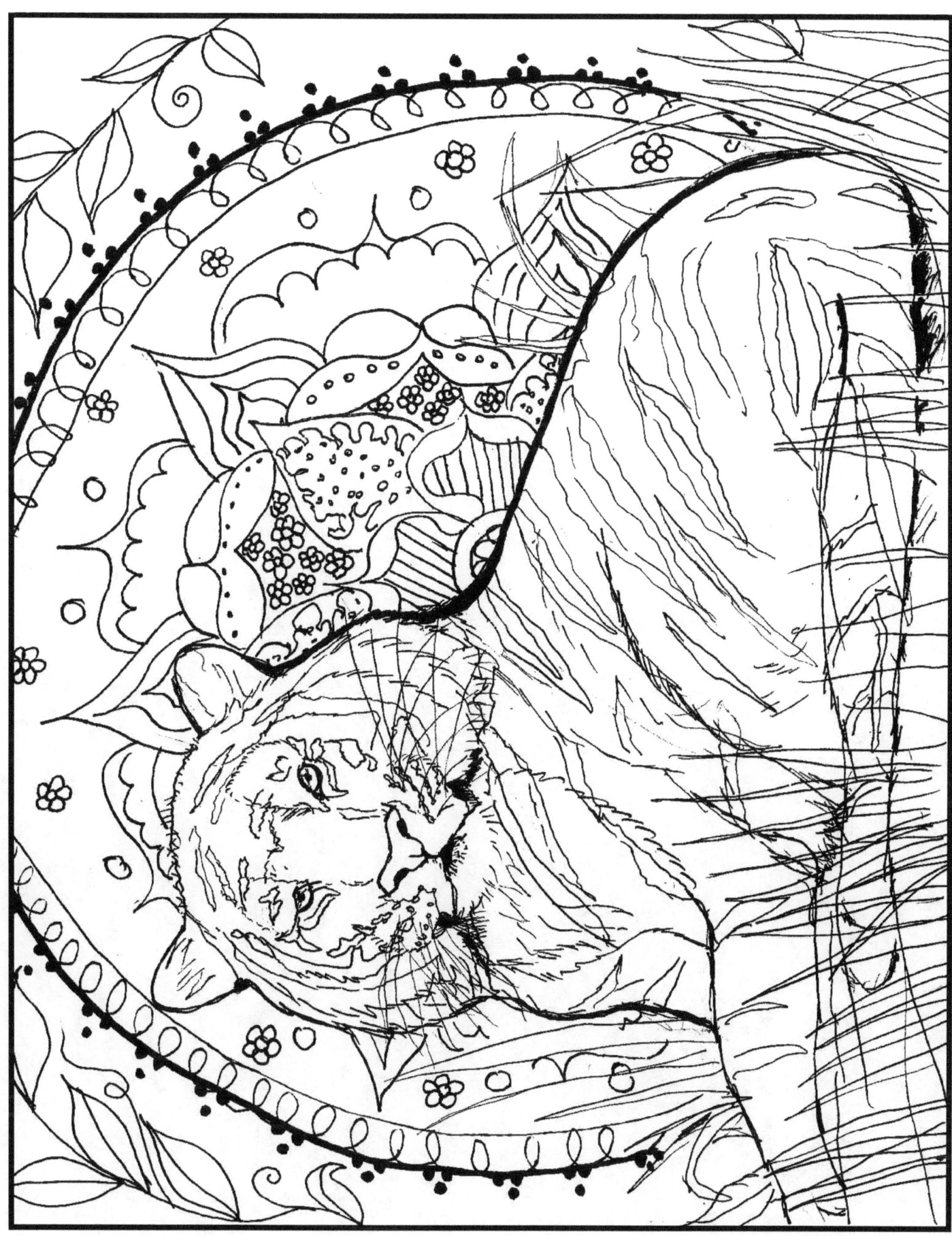

Figure 17 Tiger, Tiger

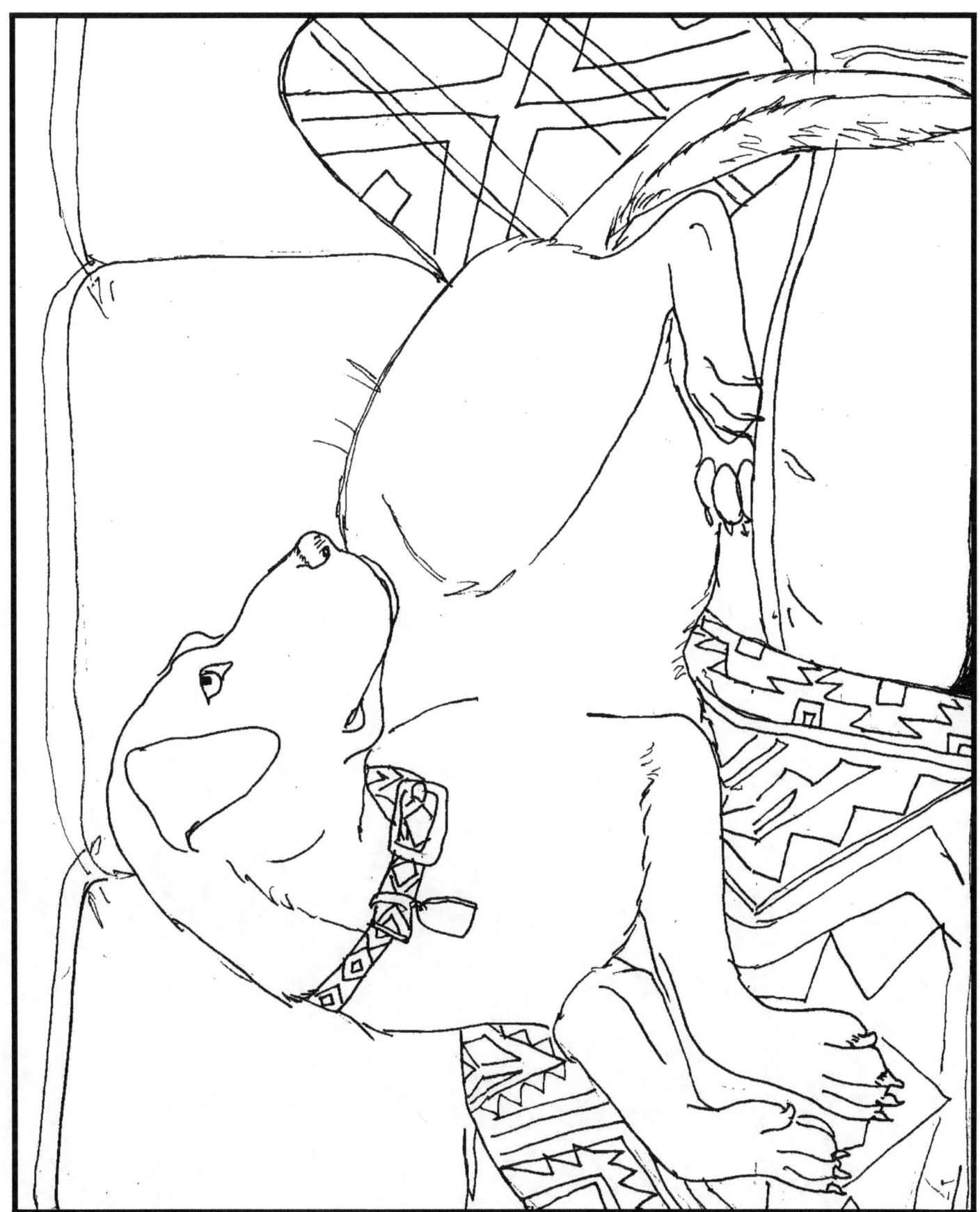

Figure 18 *Who Says No Dogs on the Furniture?*

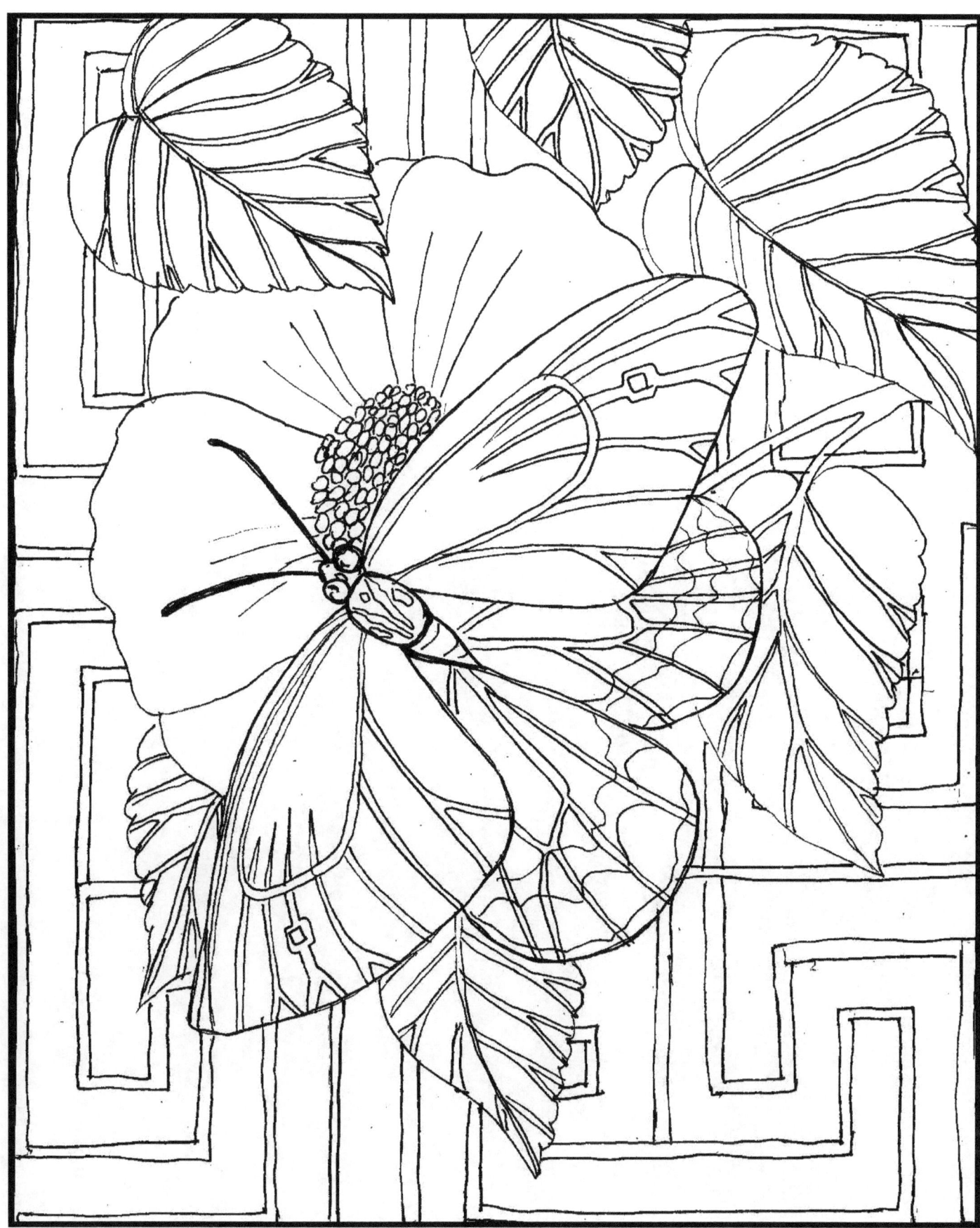

Figure 19 Butterfly

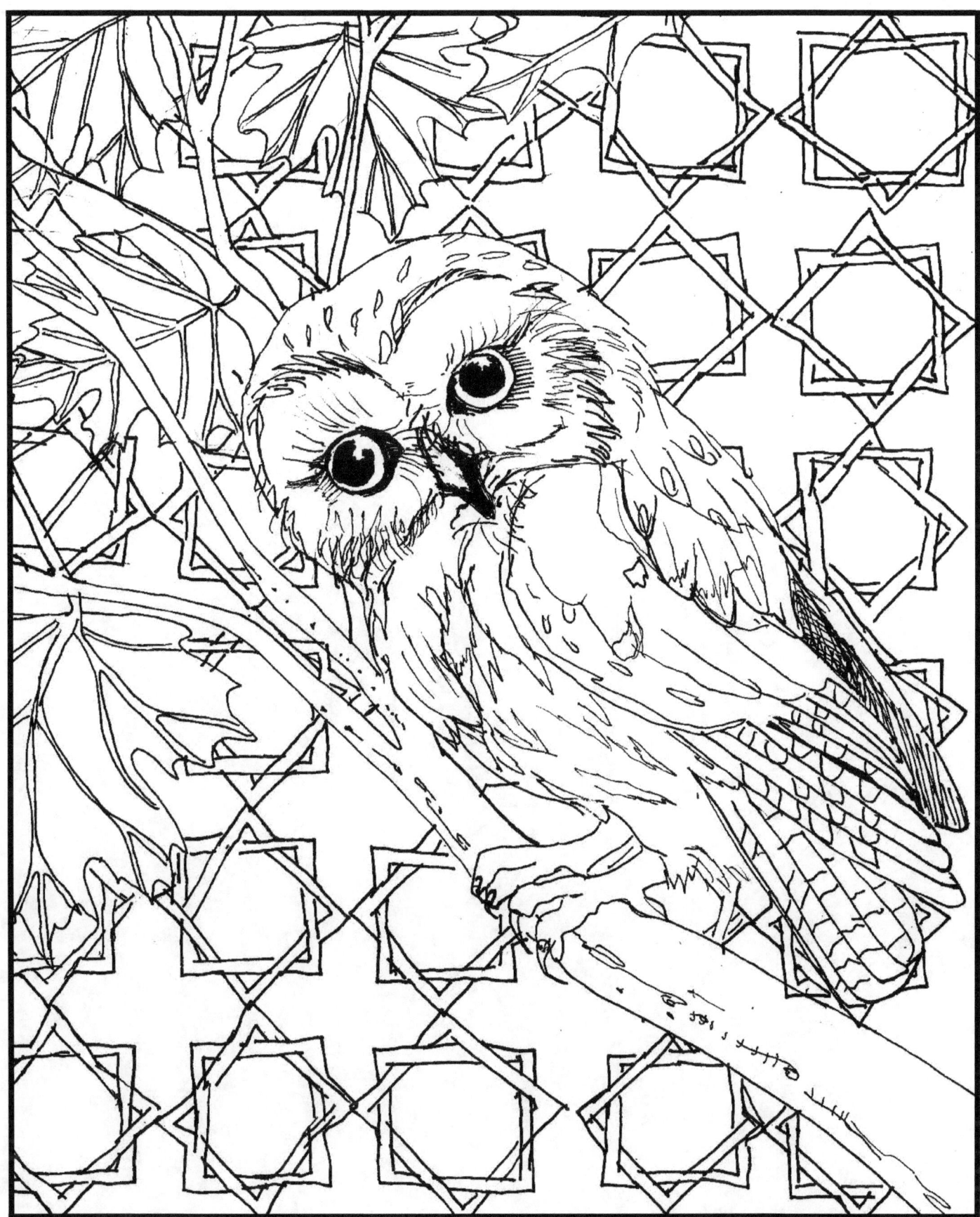

Figure 20 Saw Whet Owl

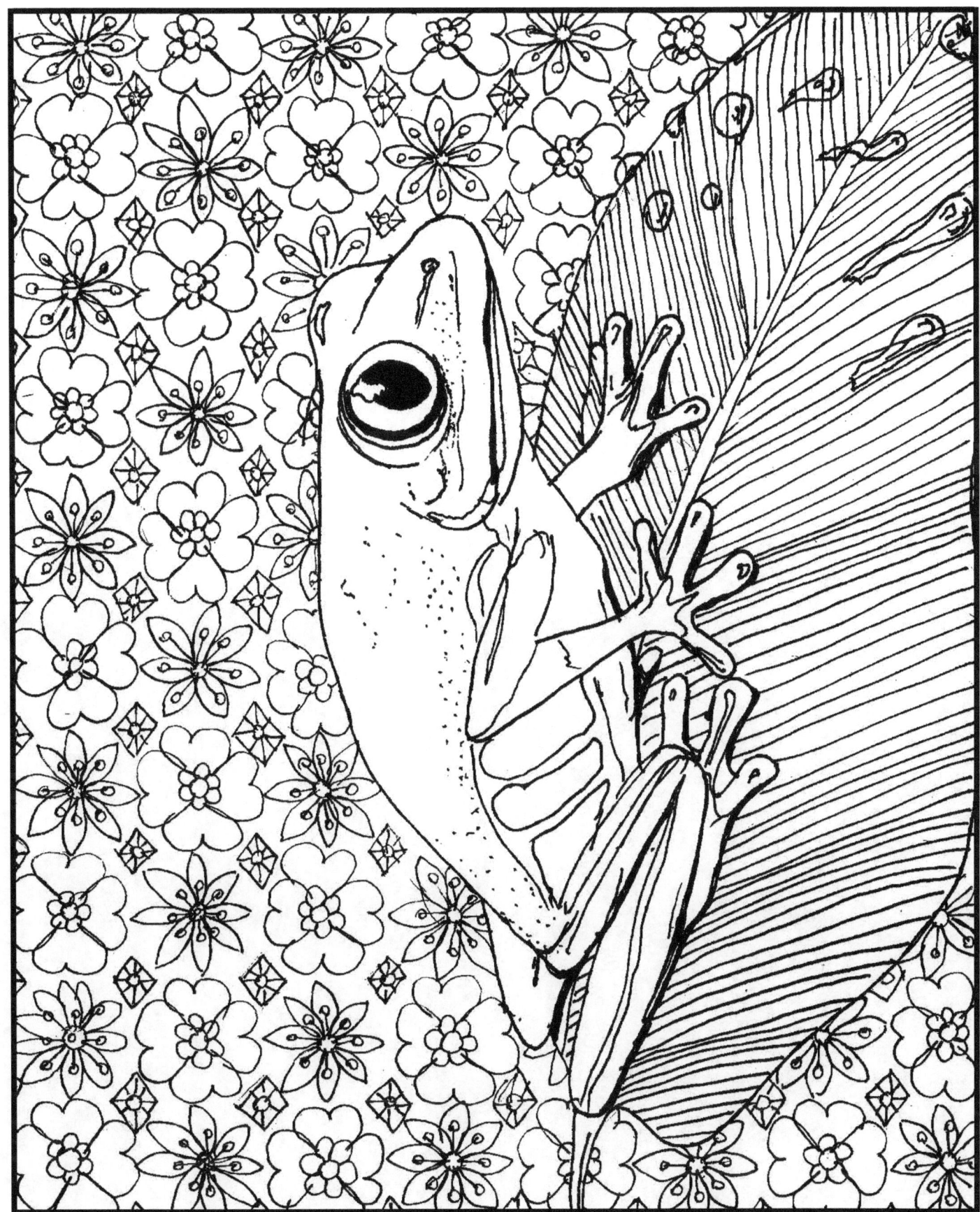

Figure 21 Red Eyed Tree Frog

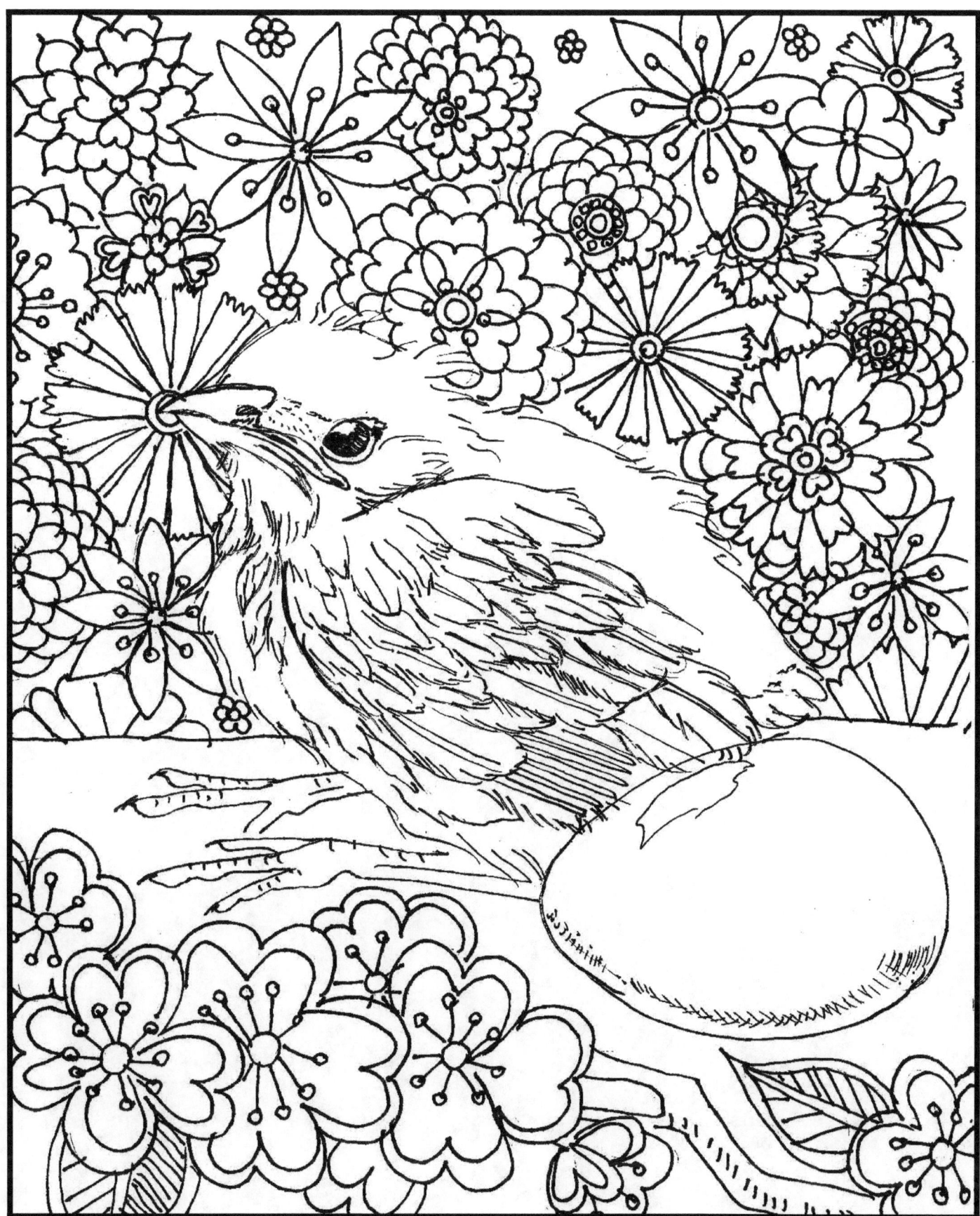

Figure 22 Baby Robin

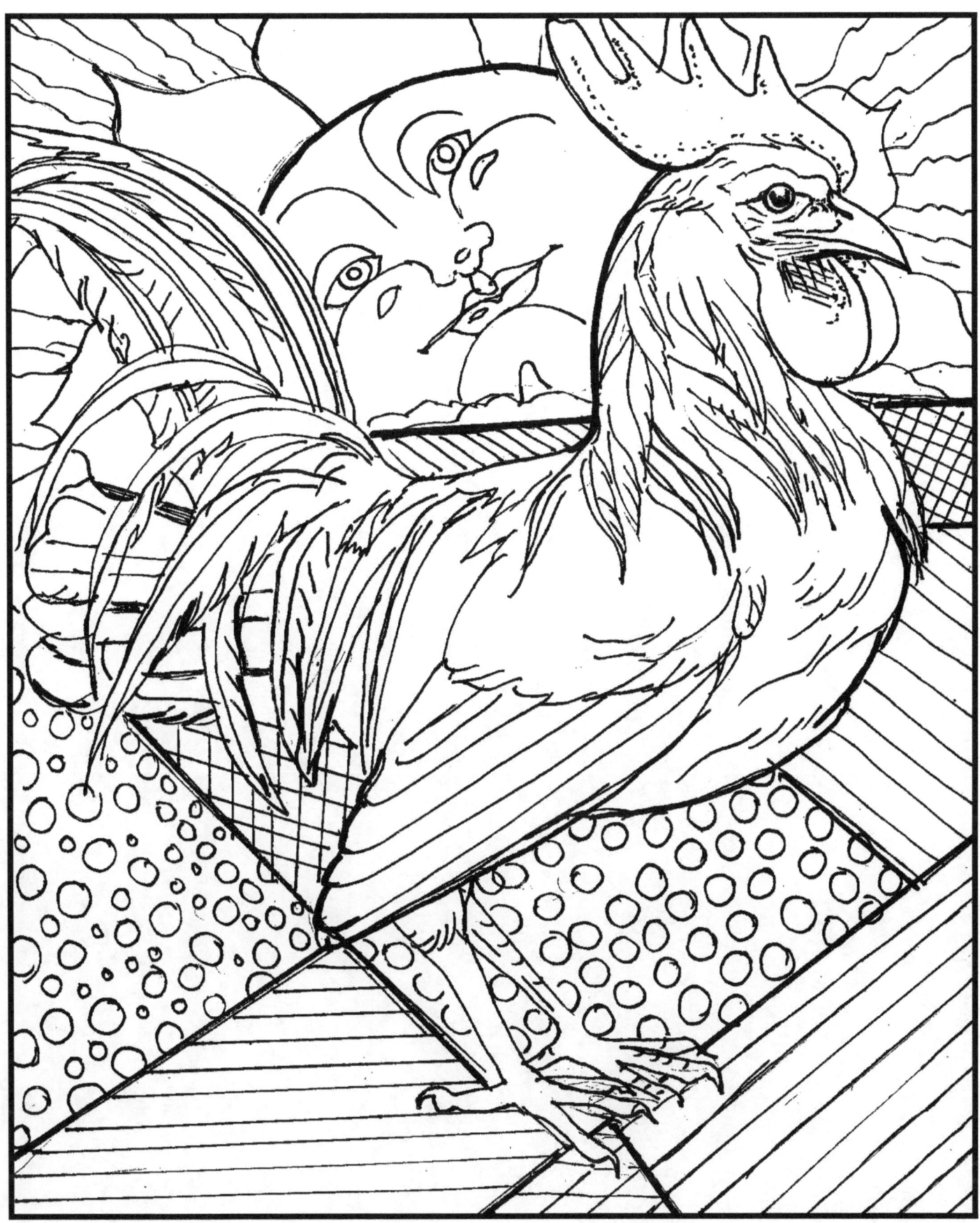

Figure 23 Up with the Sun

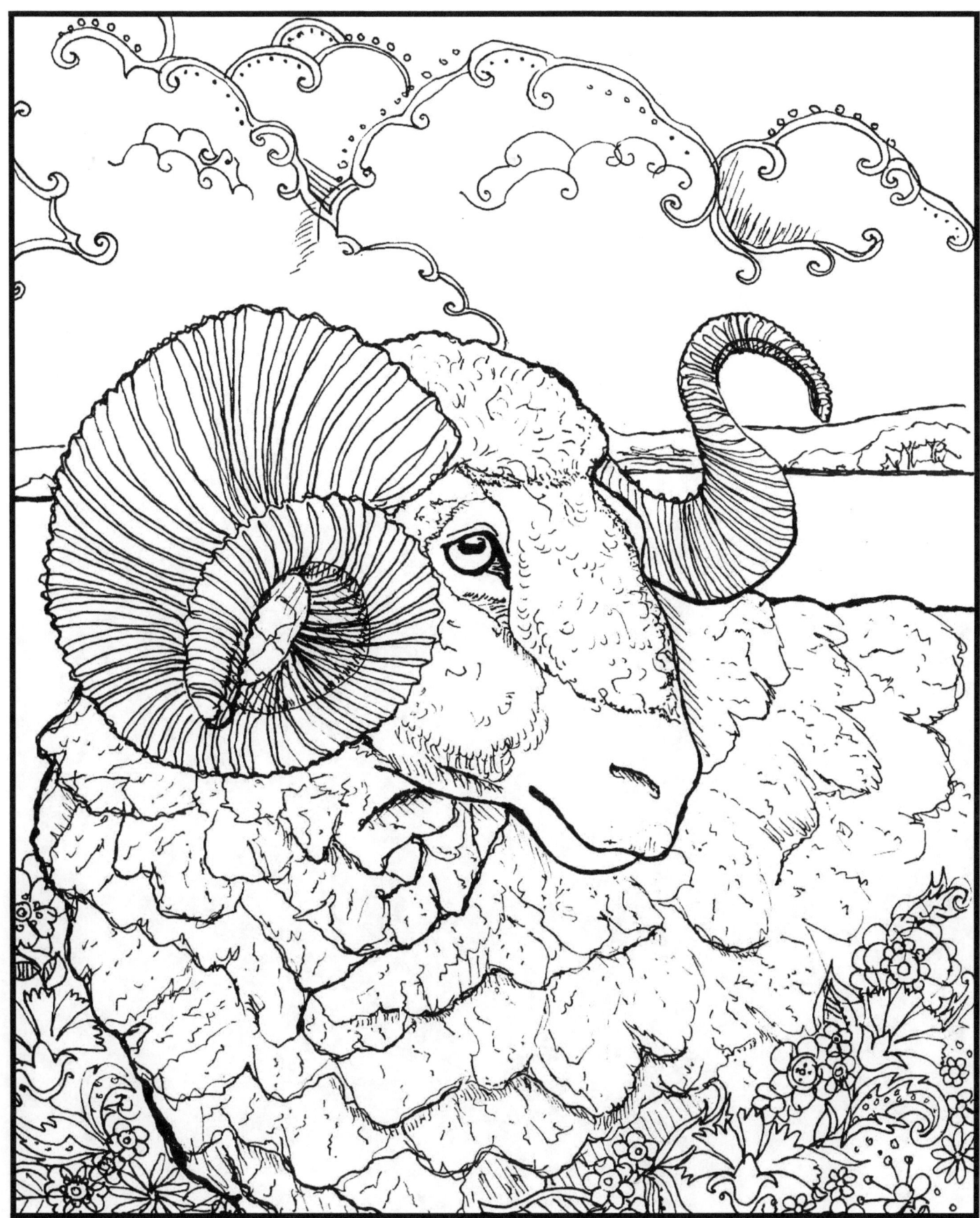

Figure 24 Merino Sheep

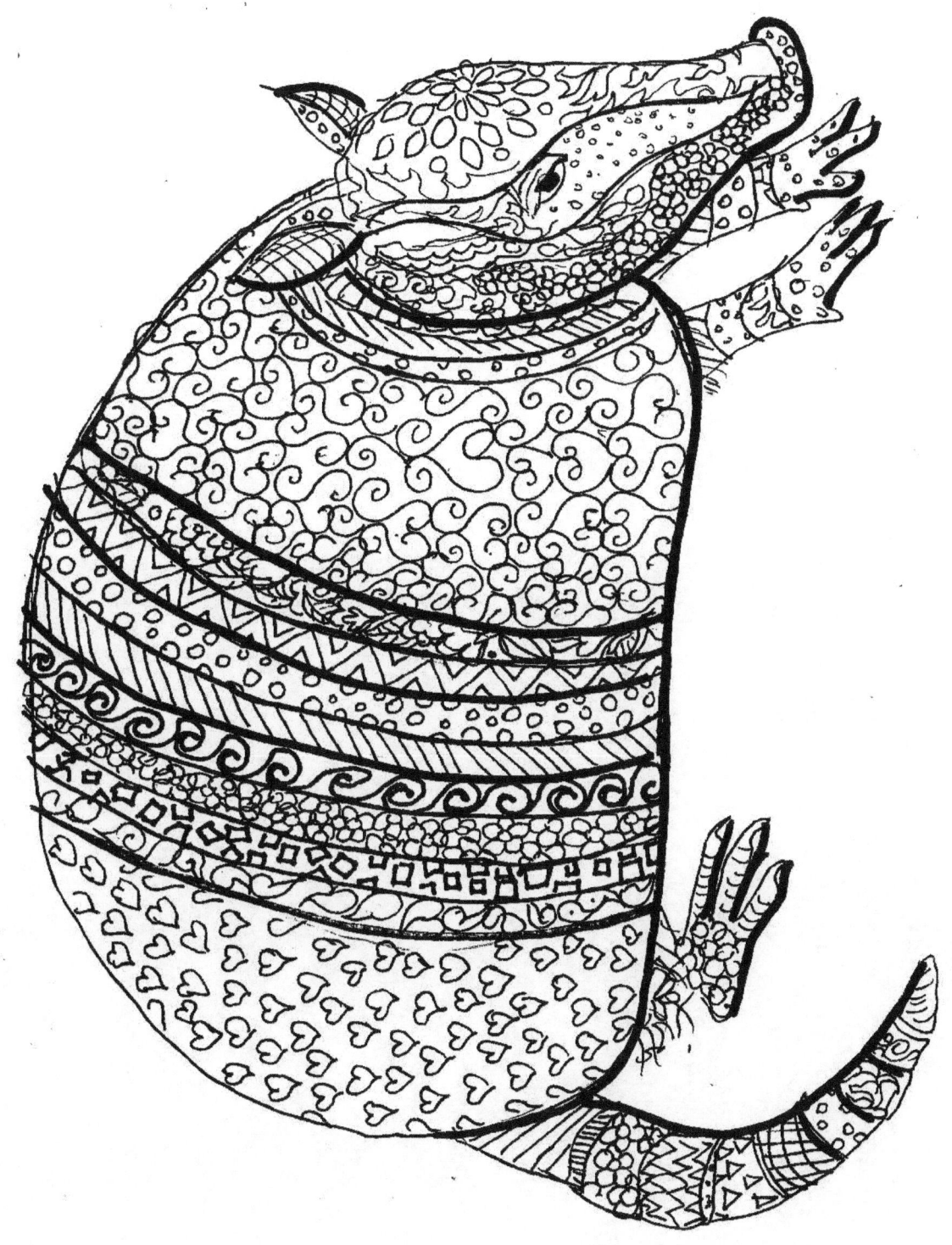

Figure 25 Armadillo

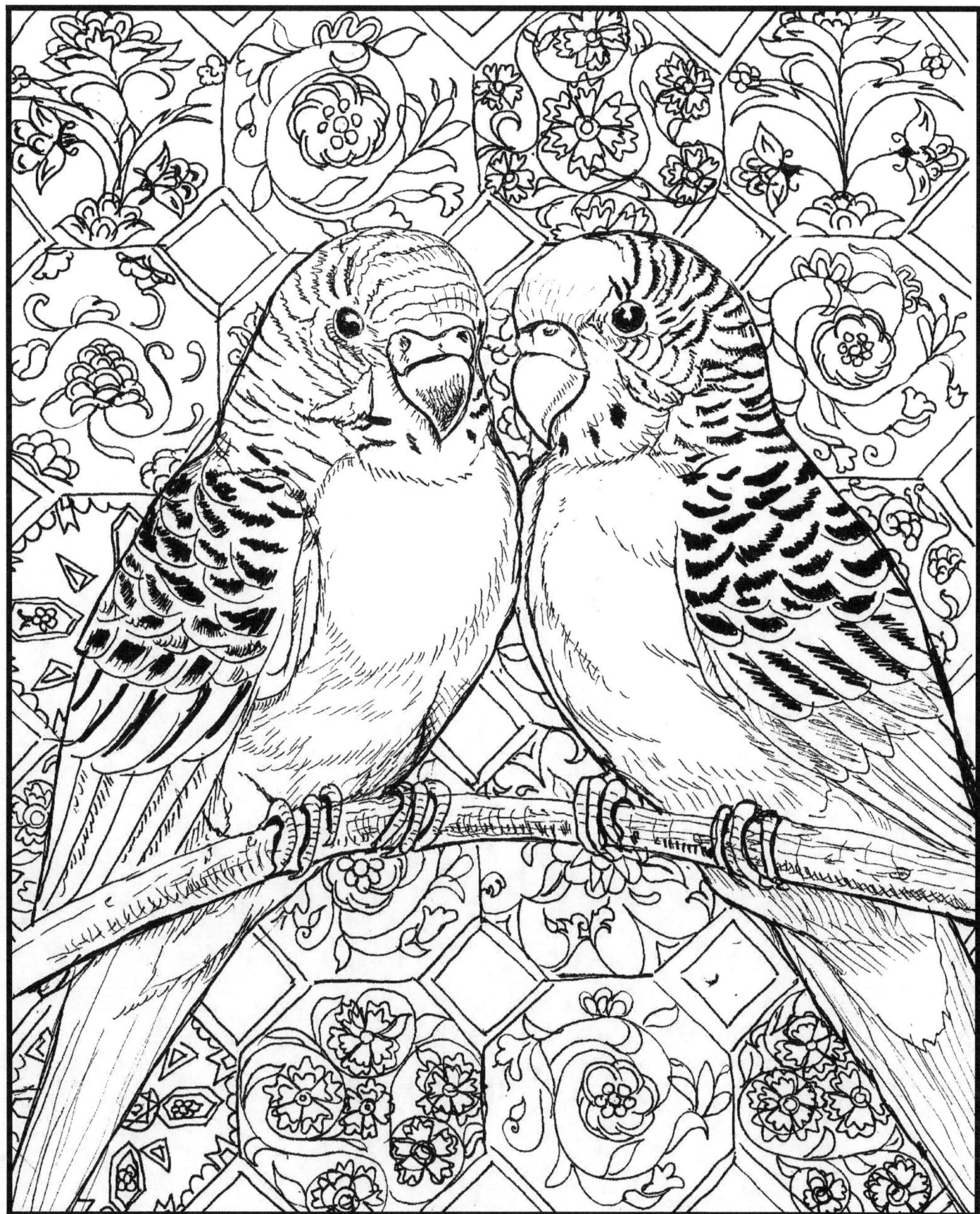

Figure 26 Budgie Buddies

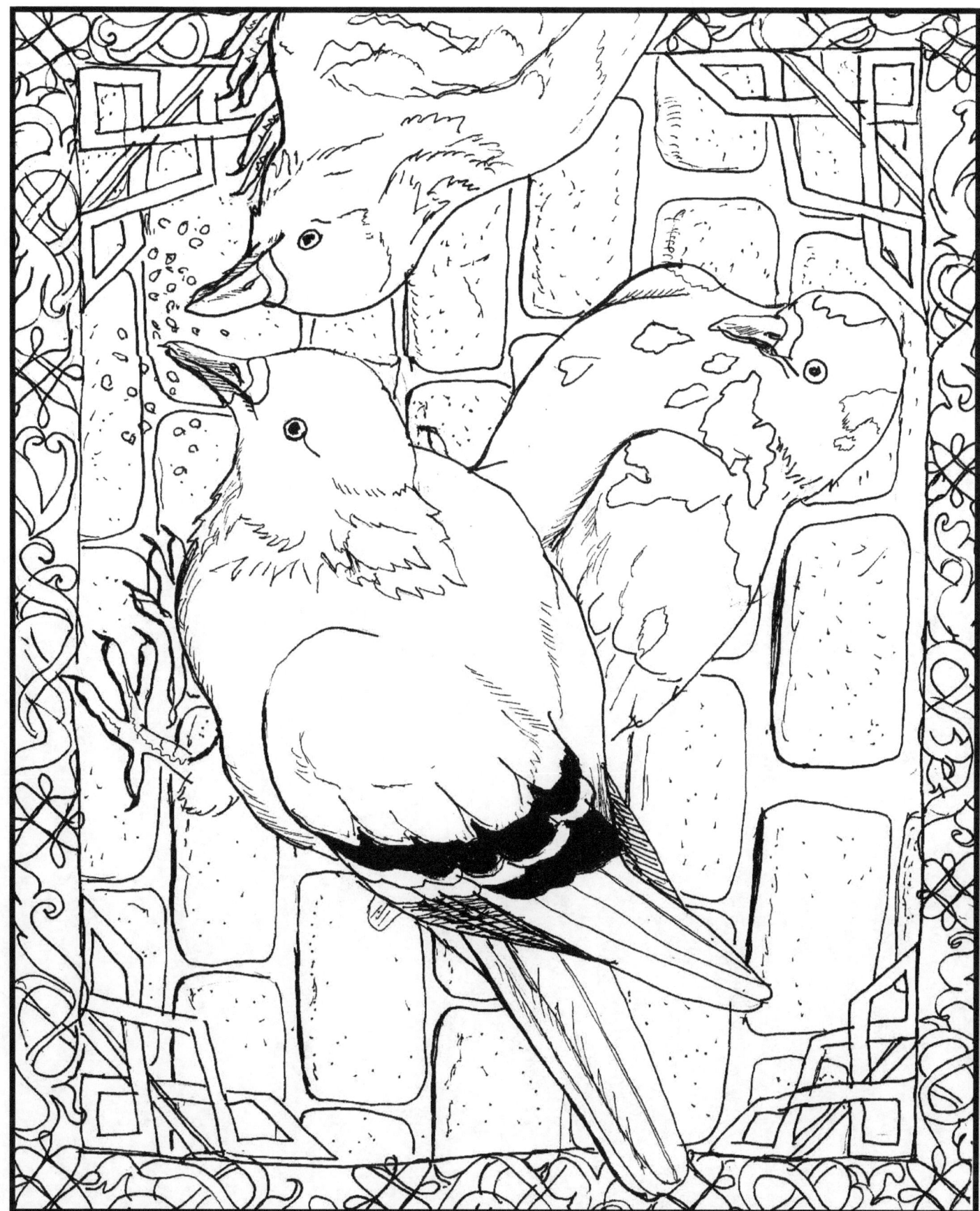

Figure 27 Dinner with Friends

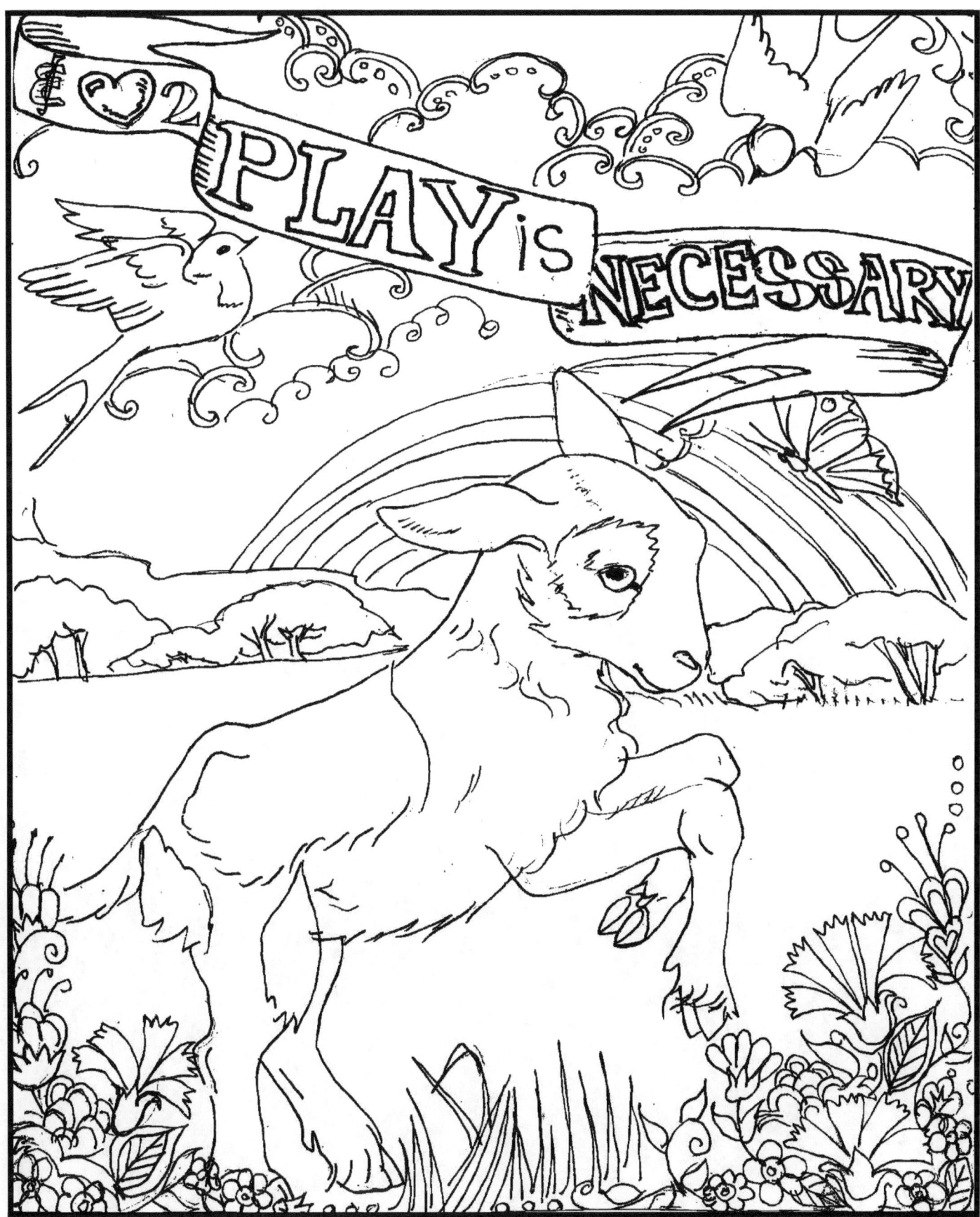

Figure 28 Playtime

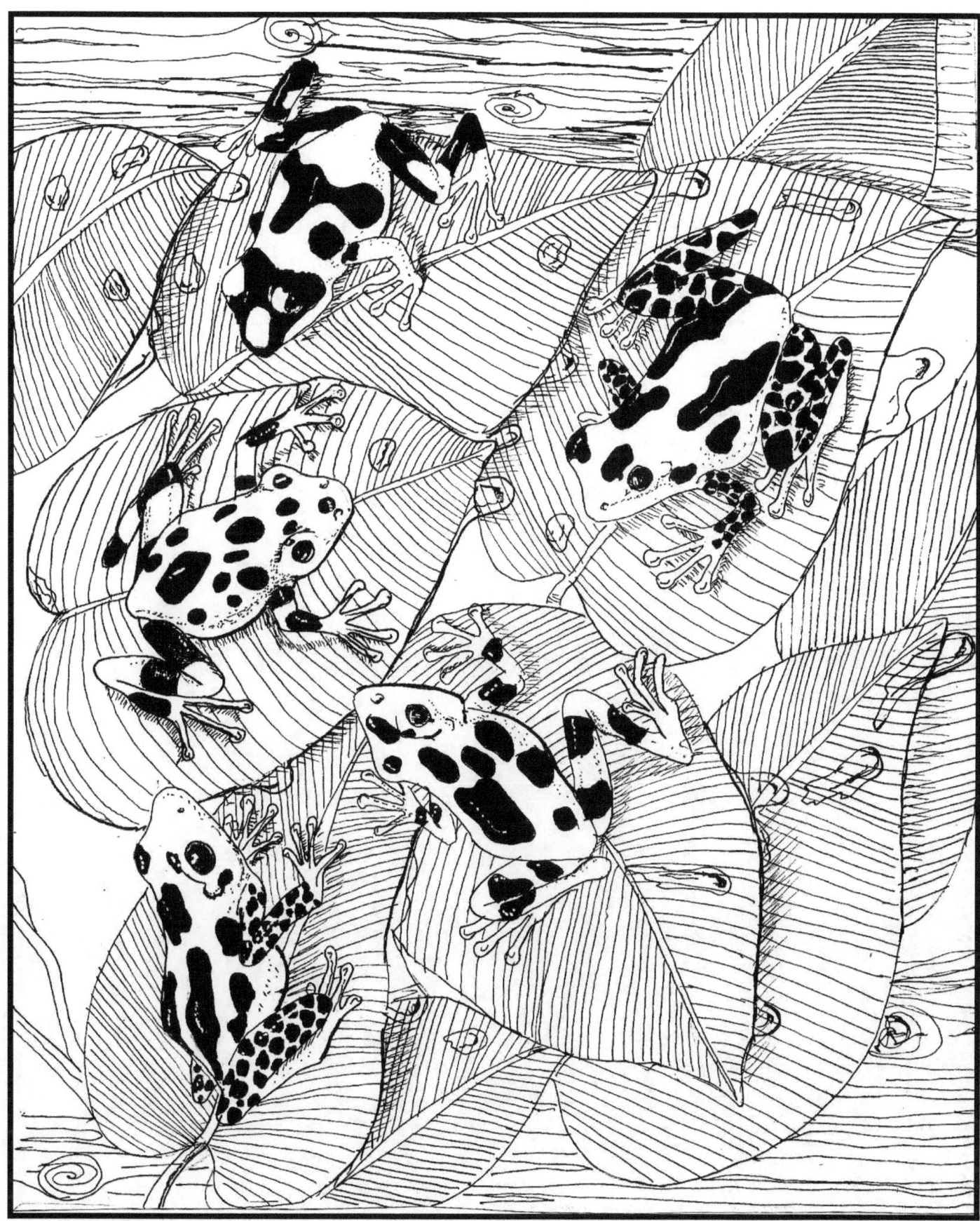

Figure 29 Rainforest Gems

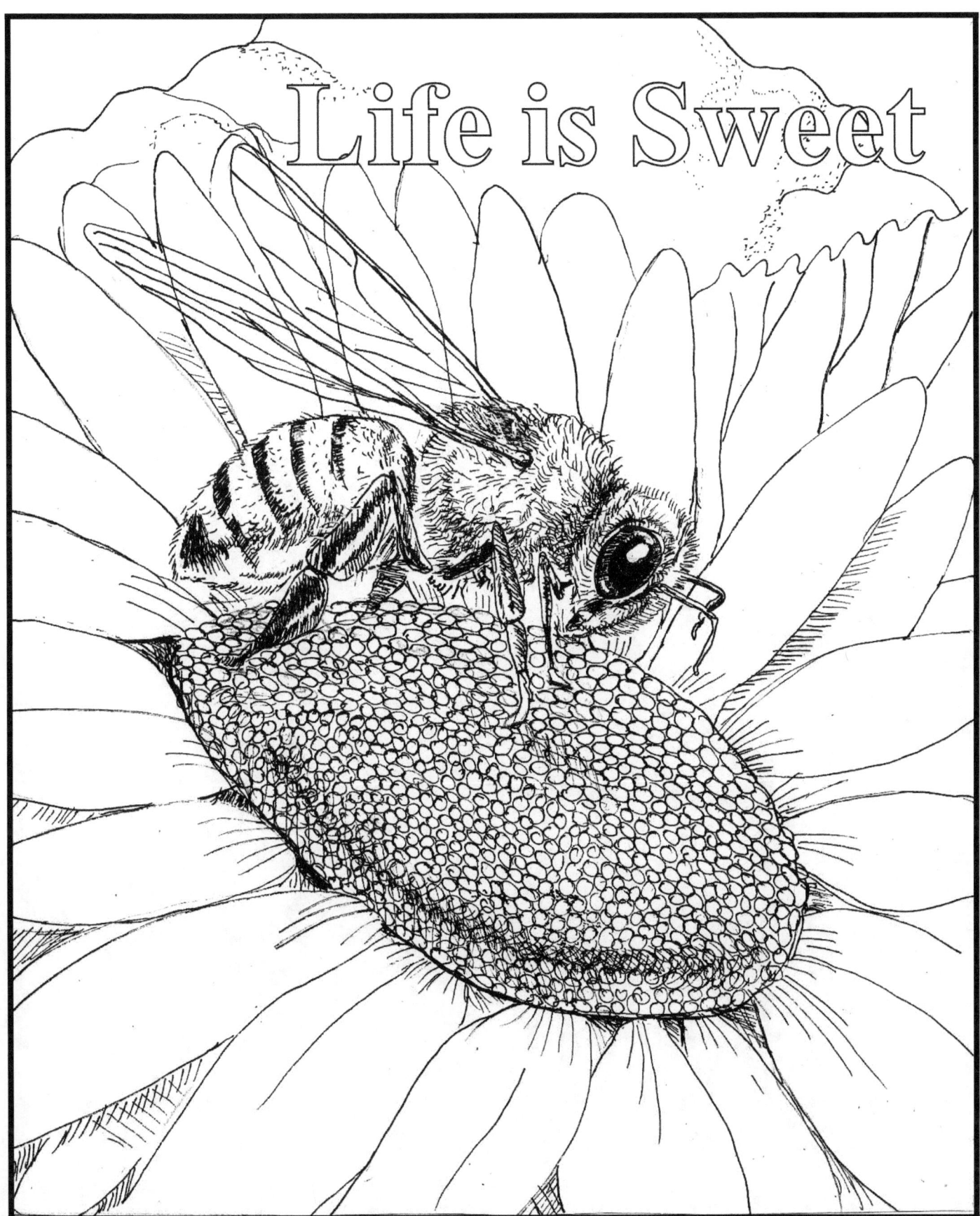

Figure 30 Life is Sweet

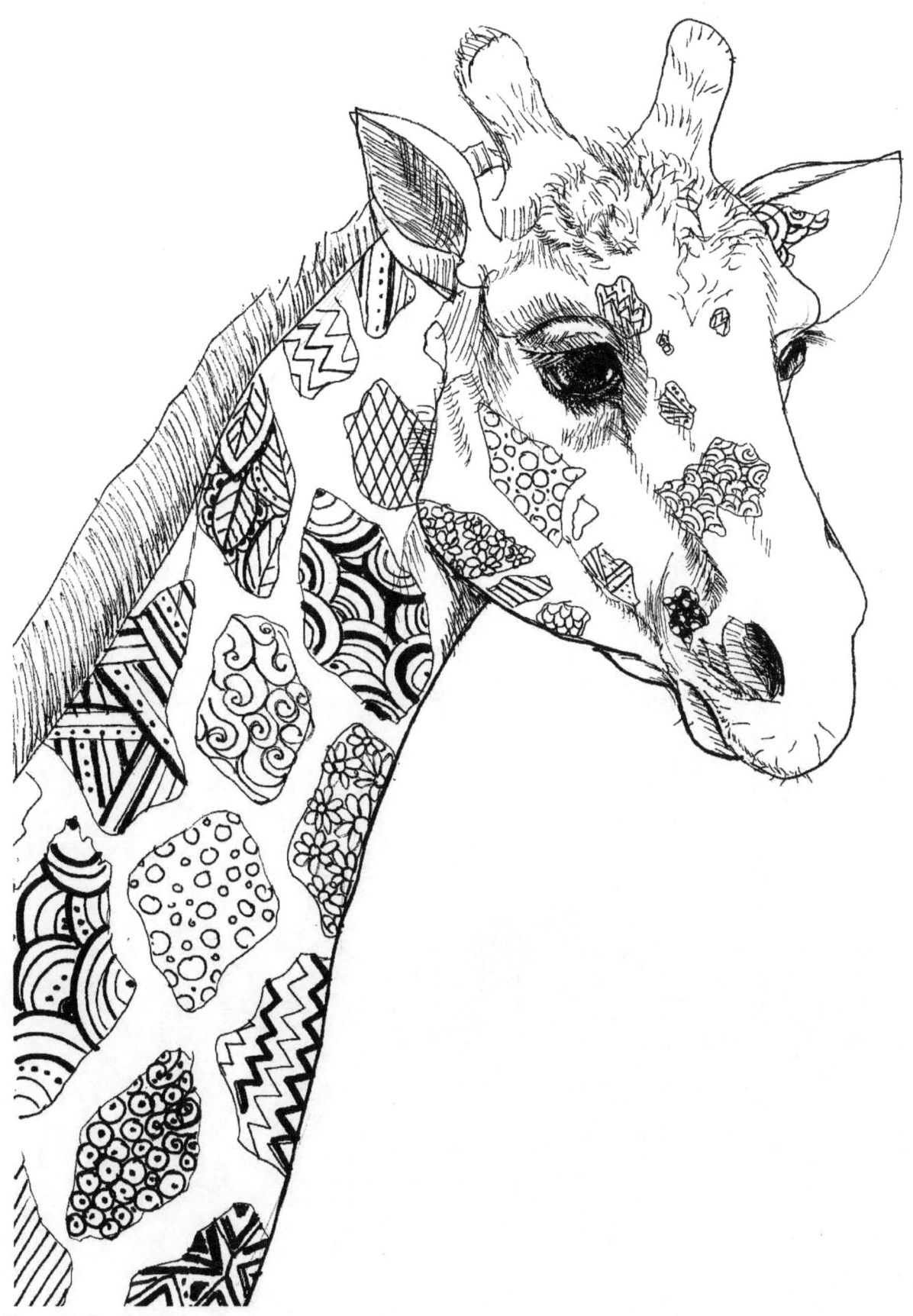

Figure 31 Giraffes

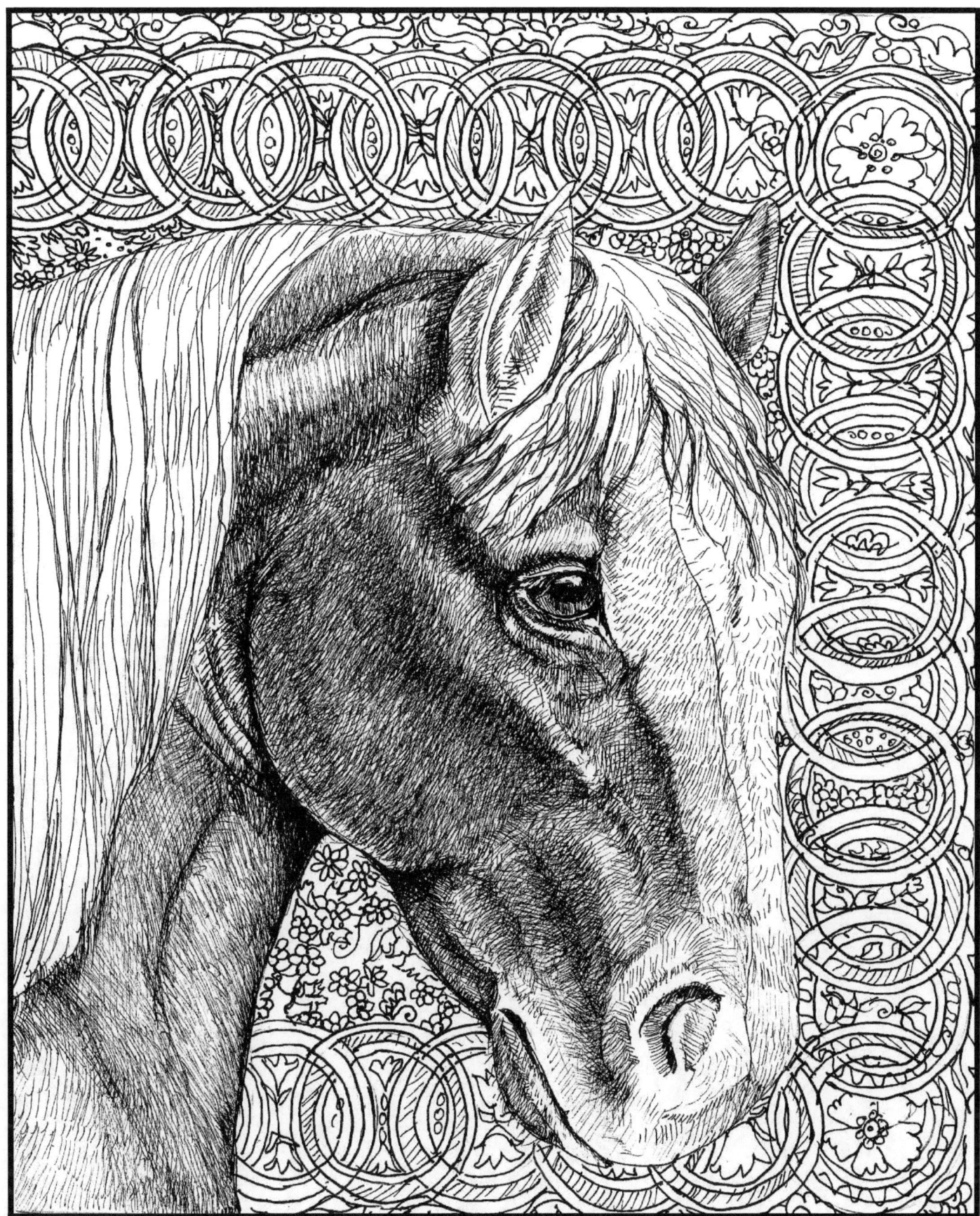

Figure 32 Horse

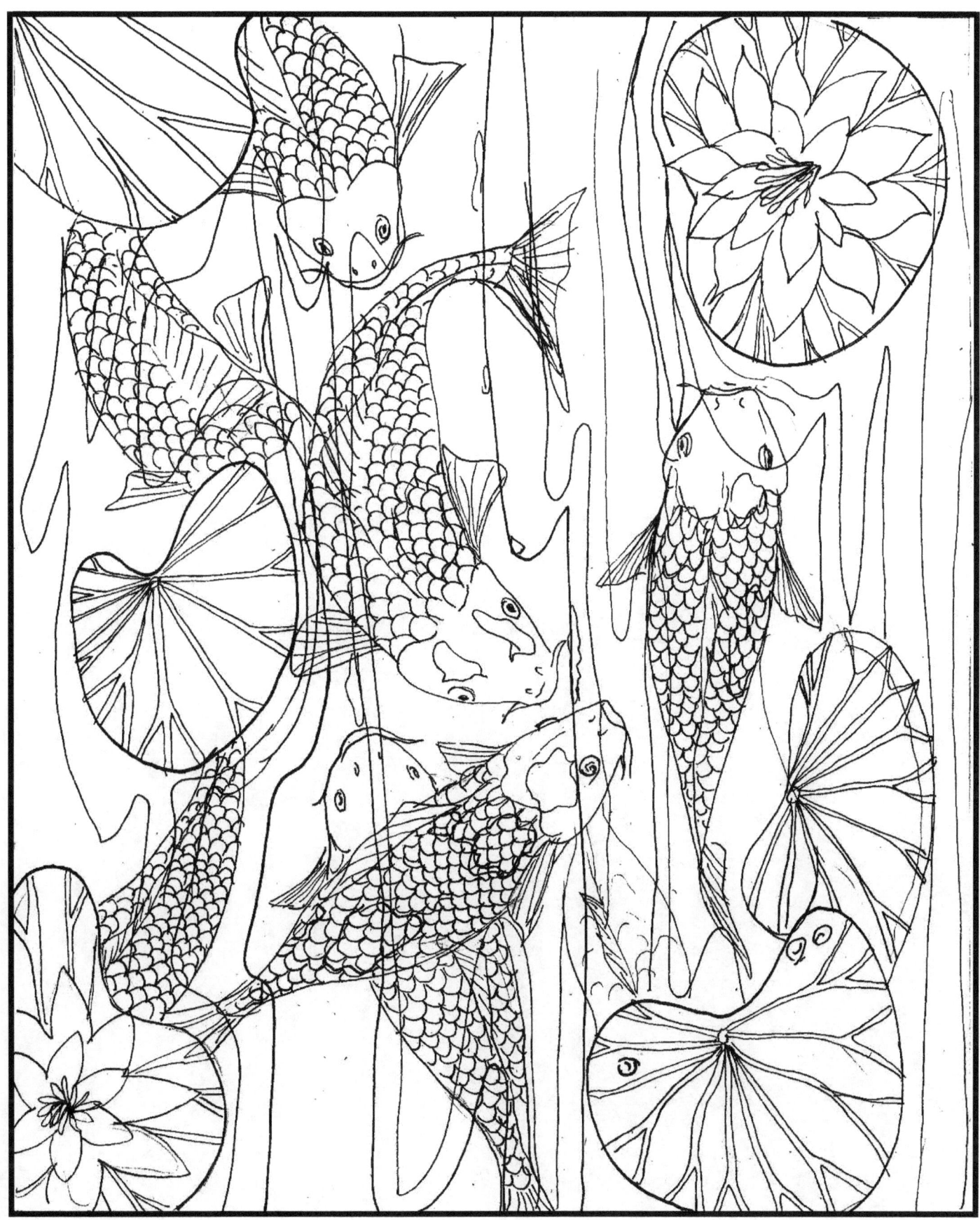

Figure 33 Koi Pond

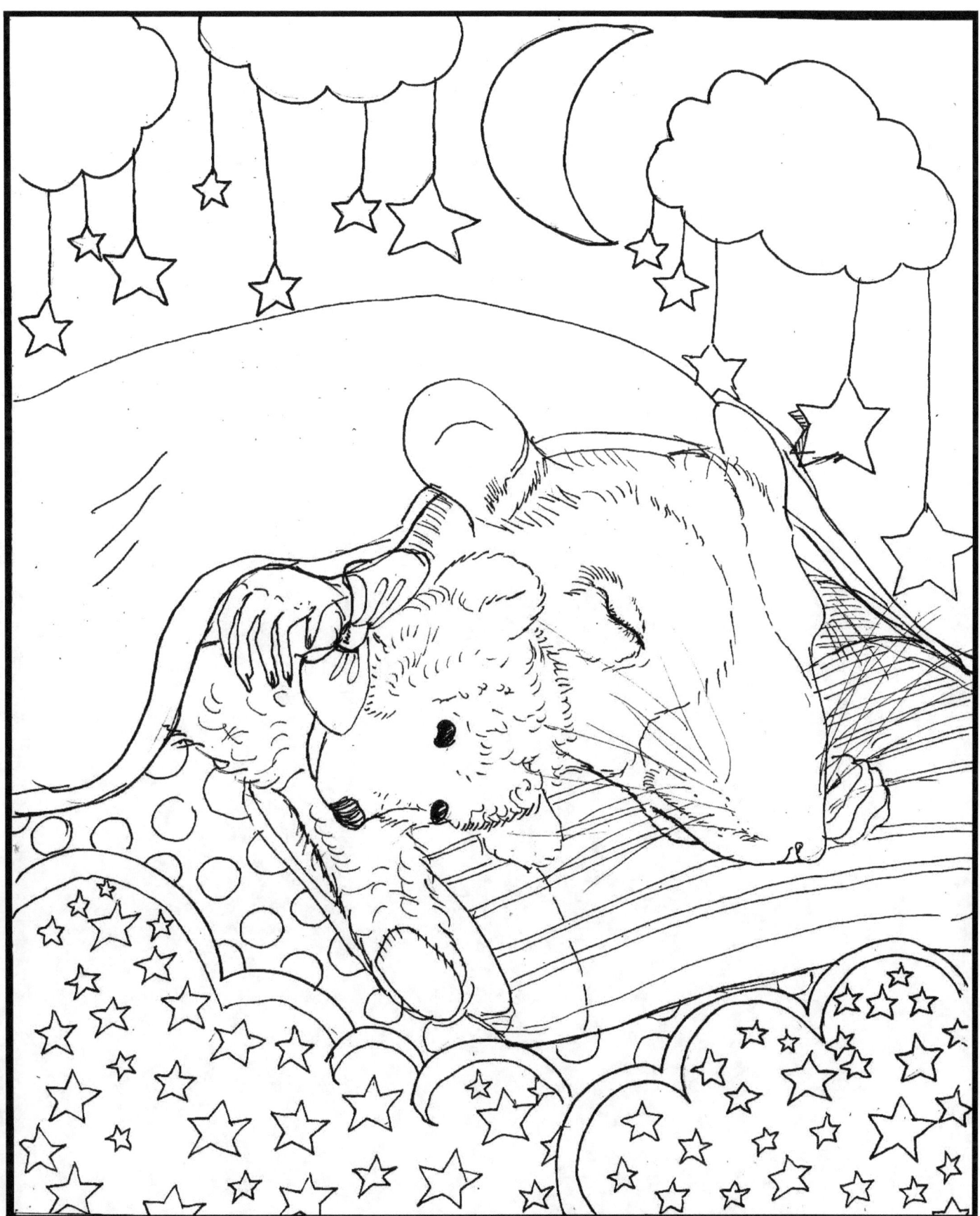

Figure 34 Sweet Dreams

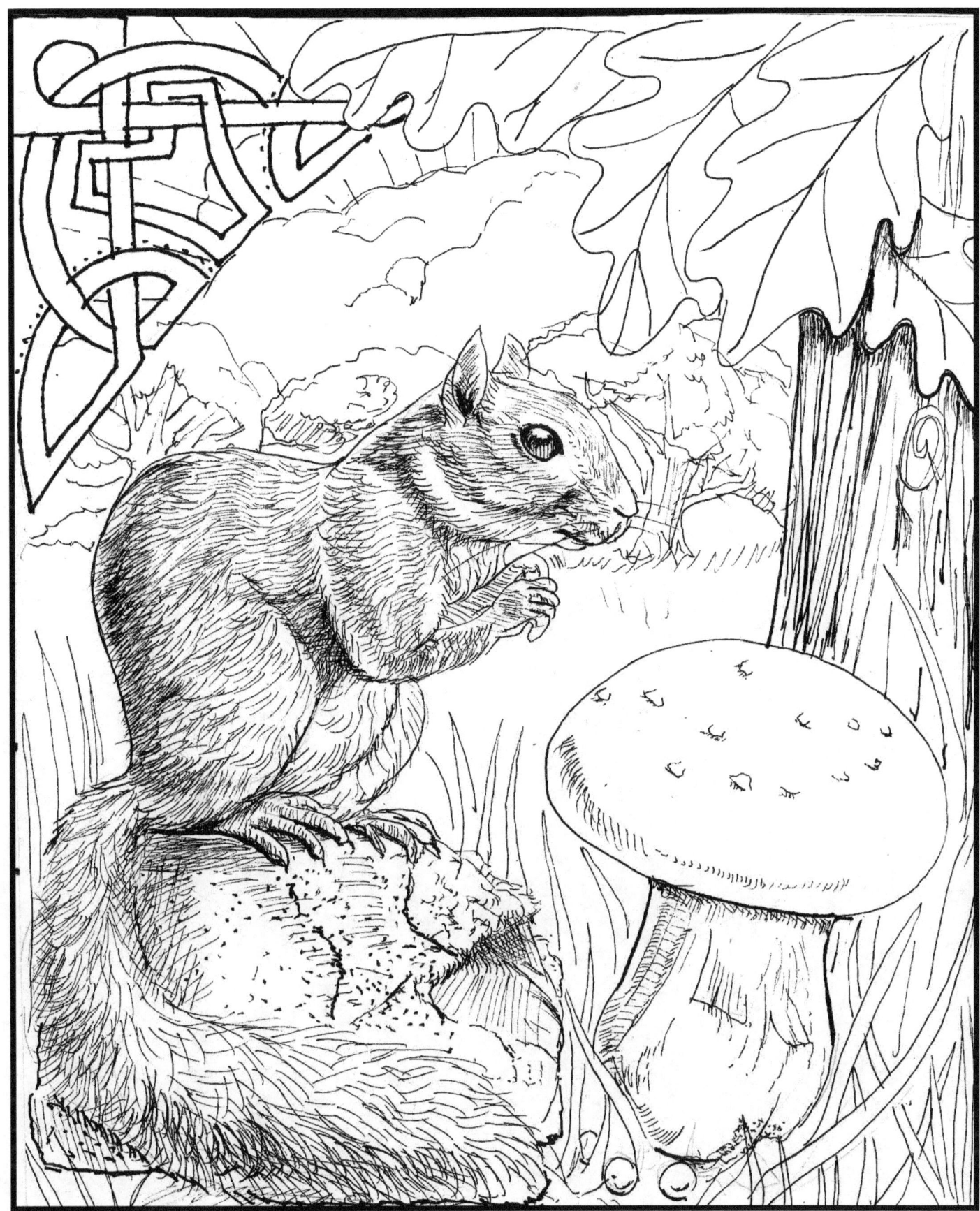

Figure 35 Will you be my friend little squirrel?

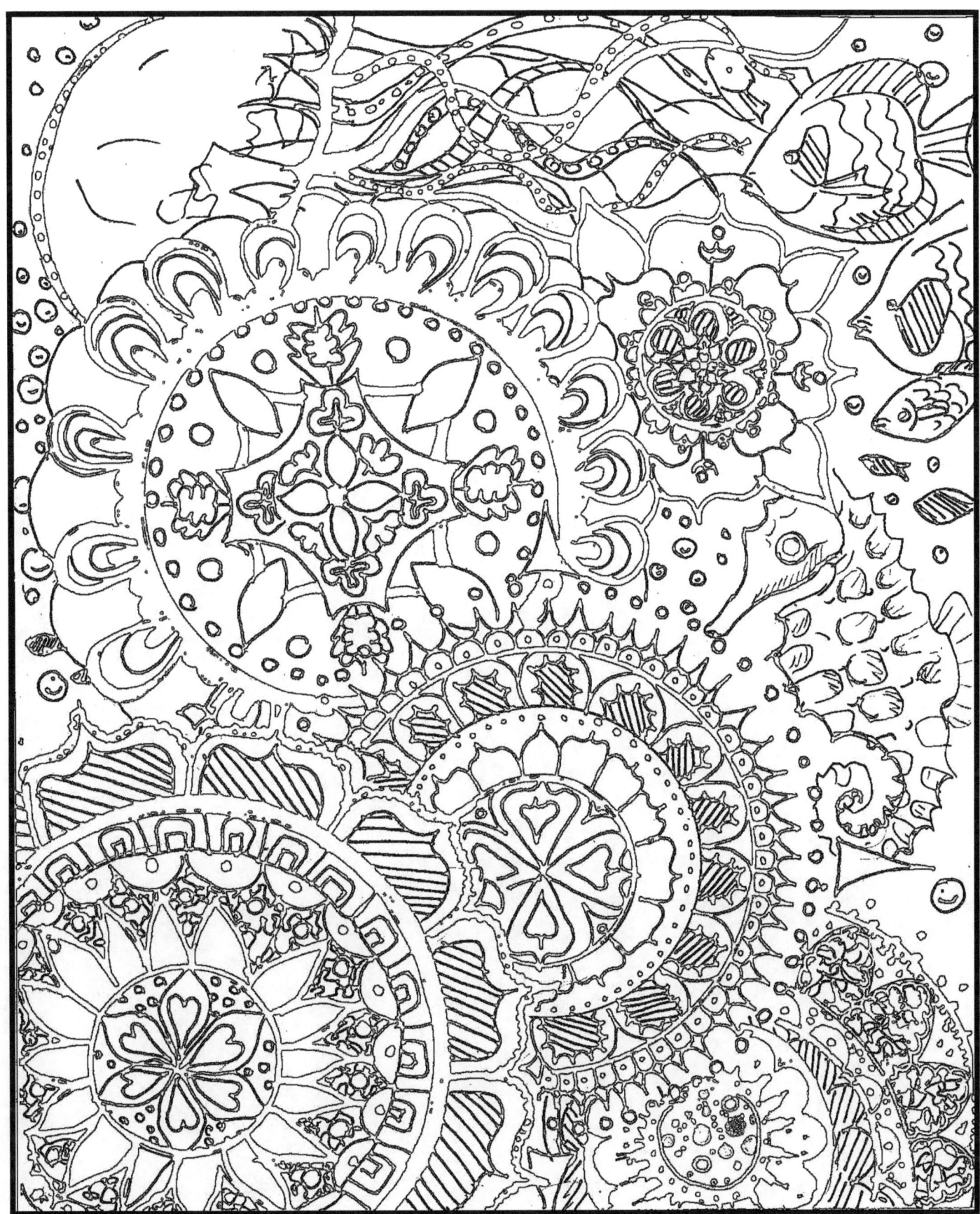

Figure 36 Ocean Mandalas

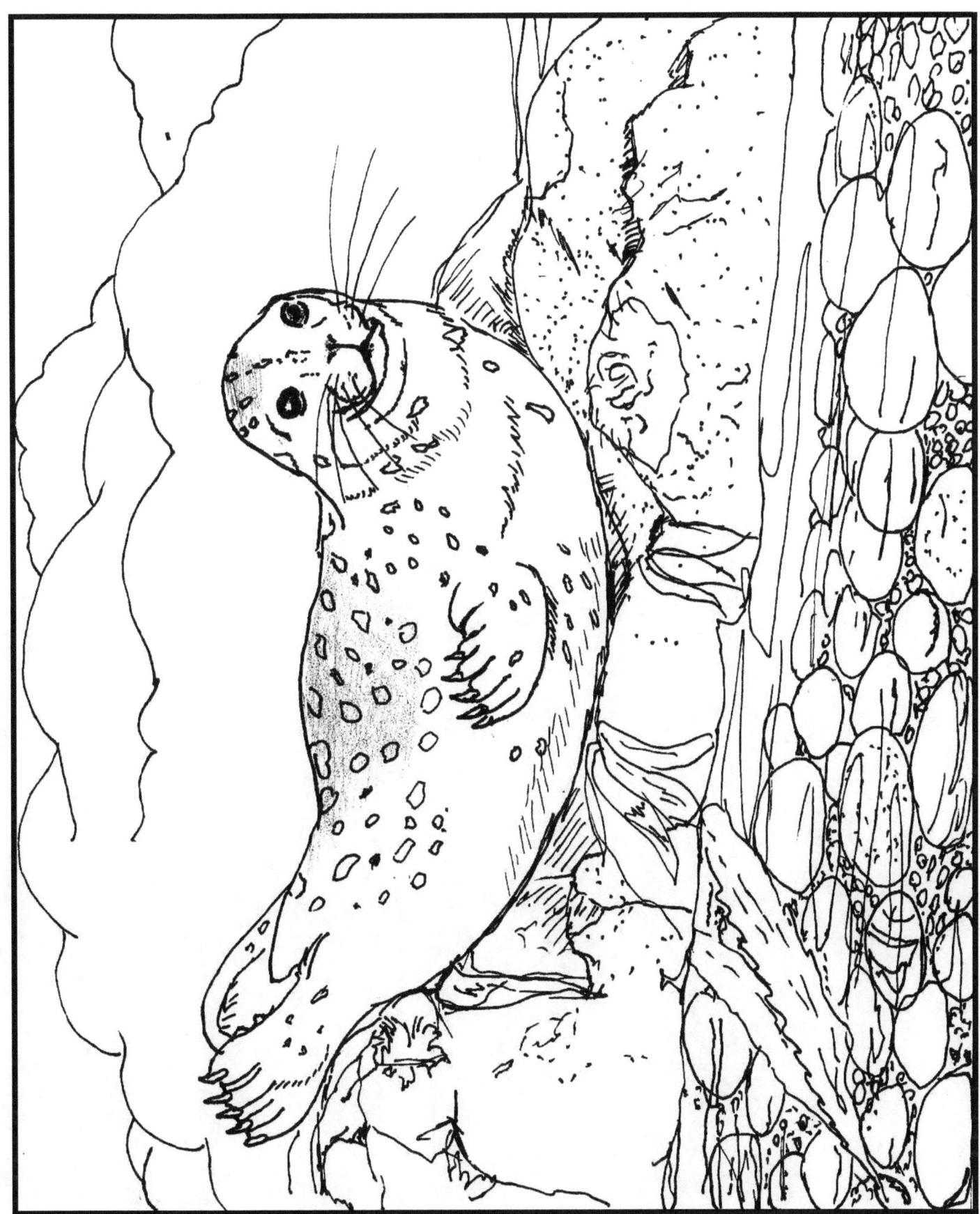

Figure 37 Harbor Seal

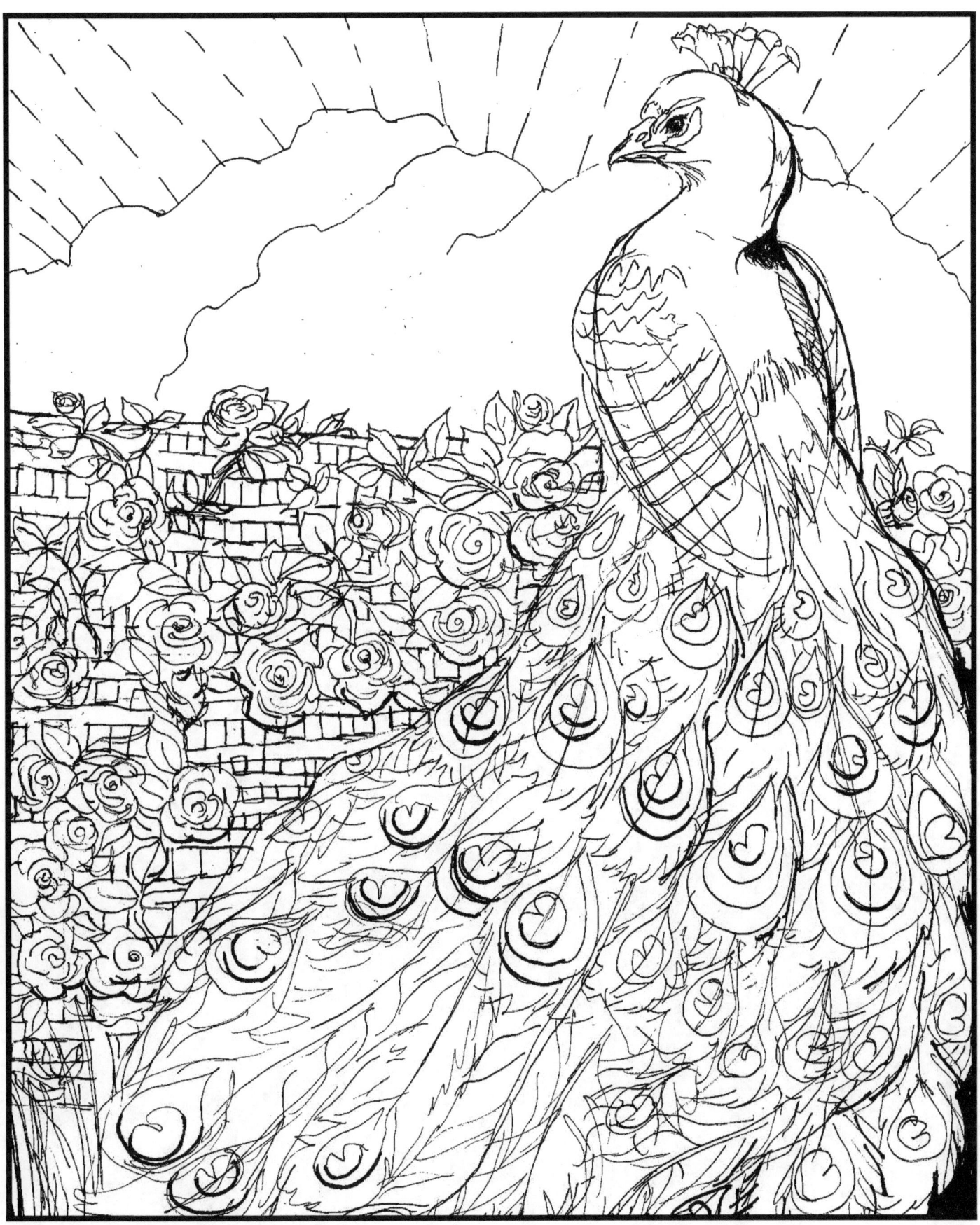

Figure 38 Morning Glory

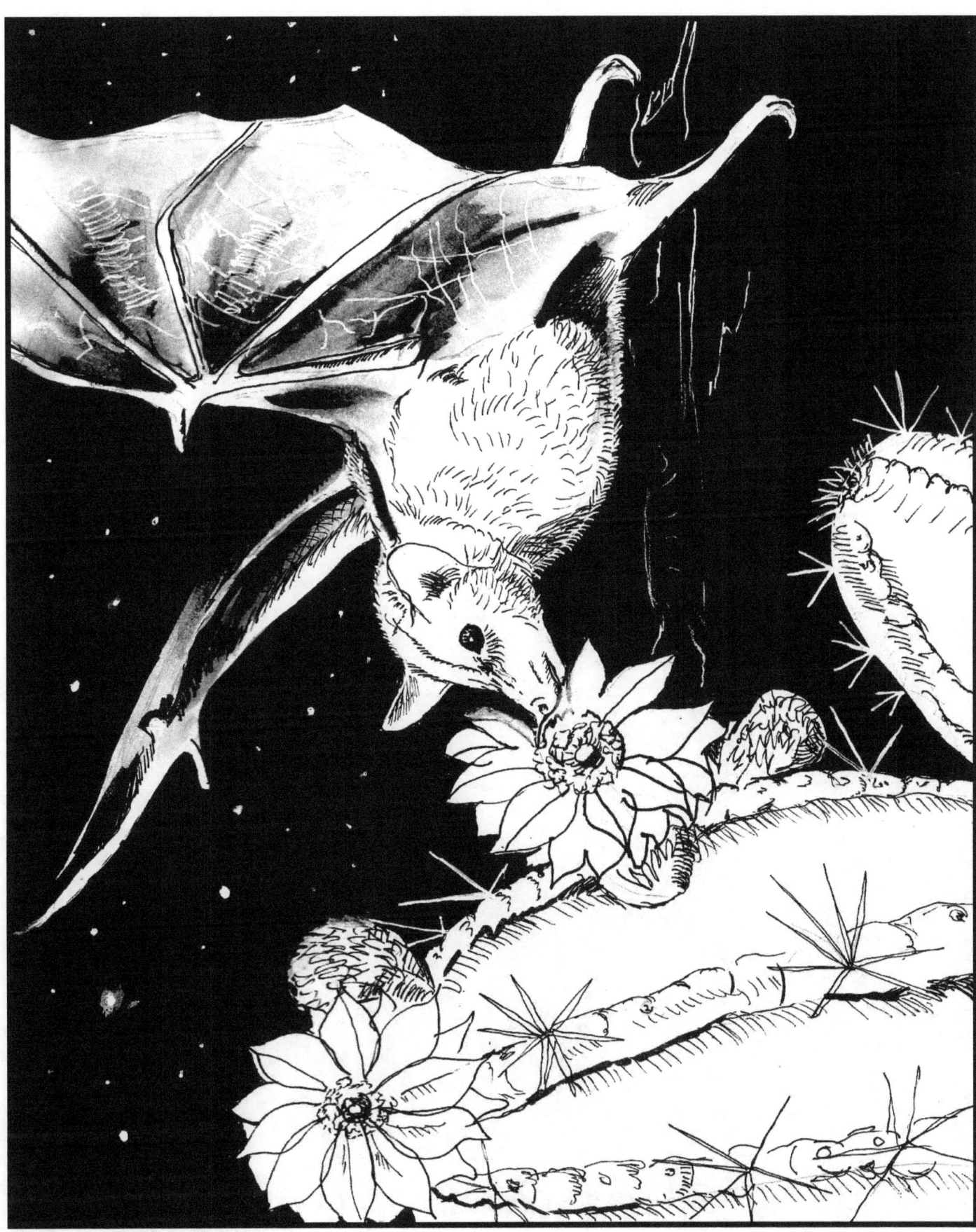

Figure 39 Midnight Snack

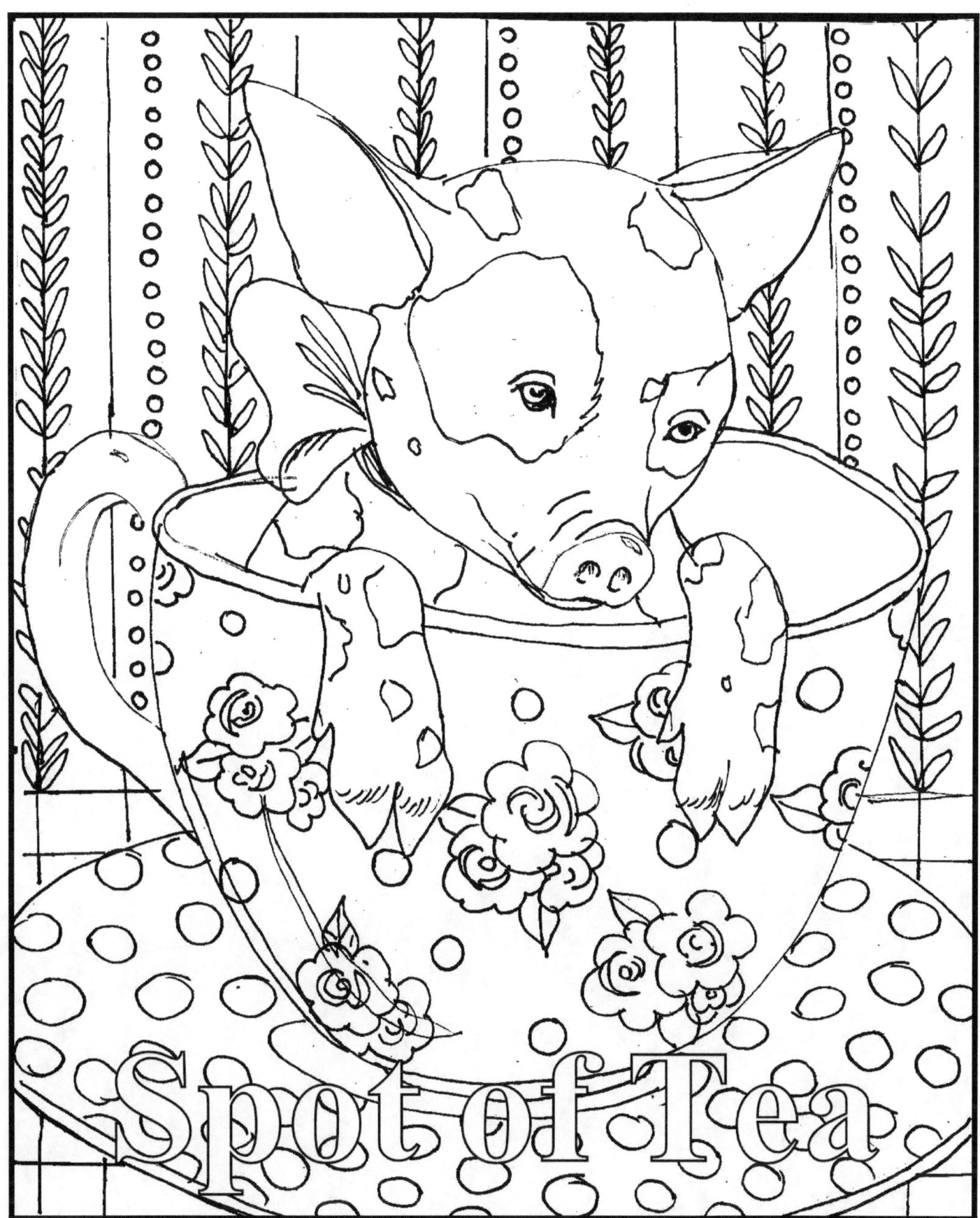

Figure 40 Spot of Tea